ISBN: 9798580693729

Cover designed by Bill Hobgood
Cover artwork by Russ Dayton
Author photography by Josephine Donatelli

Editor's Note

By the time my father's memoirs had been collected and organized into the book you begin here, I had heard many of the stories you're about to read several times. But some of them, I eagerly read for the first time during our editing process, giving me an insight into the young man I had seen in pictures and heard about as a kid.

When he asked me to be his editor, I started thinking about how in 2020, we look on the war in Vietnam with very different eyes than those of an 18-year-old kid from Elizabeth in 1967.

Whenever he and I visited a Vietnam memorial while I was growing up, he would quietly look at the walls of names, occasionally looking for someone that he knew from his home town. He explained the exhibits matter-of-factly, keeping our conversations focused on bulkheads, dog tags, and mess cooking, avoiding the politics of the war.

I recall only once that he spoke to me about Vietnam from a political perspective. While I was in my early twenties, America was losing men and women every day in Iraq and Afghanistan, quagmires of a different sort that we watched live on TV. We were discussing the war and the toll it was taking, and he got really quiet.

"When I was your age," he said, "the politicians wasted thousands and thousands of lives on a war without an end and without a clear strategy, and that's exactly what they're doing again." In his own quiet way, he was furious at having to see history repeated.

I was looking forward to reading more reflections like this on the past fifty years since he left the Navy. Dad wasn't an activist, but he clearly had opinions about the war that shaped his generation. I couldn't wait to get started.

Mostly, Dad did not write that book.

There are no references to anti-war protests, racial tensions are only discussed briefly, and there are very few musings on the plight of the North Vietnamese. That was what I thought I wanted to read about, but there is no shortage of literature or film on those subjects.

As I got further, I stopped wishing for the book he didn't write and started appreciating the one he did. You and I are treated here to a different set of stories: the perspective of a blue-collar kid, from a working-class neighborhood, who found ways to turn a stint in the wartime Pacific into a good time.

Interspersed in this text are interludes written by R.H. Small, Commander, United States Navy, who served as Captain of the

USS DuPont during my father's service. I found these to be fascinating windows into the "why" for many of the things Dad experienced on the ship. I think you will too.

There's plenty of heartache to go around about the war in Vietnam. Instead, enjoy discovering why my dad slept above-decks for four months. Look forward to maybe the dumbest A.W.O.L. story you've ever heard. And in the midst of all these, you'll even read some sections that make your blood run cold or your eyes well up. I know they did mine.

-Bobby Perrotti
2020

I won't tell the story the way it happened. I'll tell it the way I remember it.
-Finn as written by Mitch Glazer, from the film *Great Expectations (1998)*

Author's Note

It has taken me fifty years to collect these experiences into one volume. My first thought to document my time in the Navy started in 2010, when my ship, the *USS DuPont DD-941,* held its first informal reunion in Alexandria, Virginia. Reuniting with my old shipmates opened up a floodgate of memories for me, and little by little, I wrote most of these stories down, sharpening the details as I could verify with the others who were there.

While I begin in 1966, it was several years before then that first got me thinking about joining the Navy.

My Uncle was a sailor that served in World War II, and my admiration for him surely influenced my decision to enlist. While I can't really recall a time *before* wanting to join the Navy, I think my first inkling really came after watching Abbott and Costello's *In the Navy*. I thought to myself, *I can do that!*

The stories in this book took place a long time ago, but I was there for every bit of it. Time did not dull my memory of the time I spent in the U.S. Navy.

All stories contained are told as accurately as I am able to remember, with fifty years of hindsight. Anyone named specifically is either named with permission, or their names have been changed to protect their privacy.

This book is dedicated to the officers & crew of the USS Dupont, with whom I served from 1967-1969. Their hard work, sacrifice, and good humor got me through three years of service during a tumultuous time for the US Military.

Thanks to Bill Hobgood for cover design, Russ Dayton for his painting of the DuPont, and Josephine Donatelli, for her portrait of the author.

Thanks to Kristin and Dana, my daughters, for the encouragement I needed to write my memoirs. Special thanks to my son and editor, Bobby, for his tireless attention to details, support, and guidance in getting this book published.

Special Thanks to Robert H. Small, Captain USN (ret), who captained the DuPont through two tours in Vietnam. His report, Comments on an East Coast Destroyer's Vietnam Tours, *provided valuable context during research and editing.*

Thanks to Kristin, Danny, Joe, Rick and Gary for their helpful feedback during the revision process.

Extra special thanks to my wonderful wife, Ginny. Without the Navy, I would never have met you, and that makes it all worth it.

-Ray

1

Decision Time
March, 1966

In the spring of 1966, the war in Vietnam was heating up, and the draft was on everyone's mind. My public high school in Elizabeth, NJ was an all-boys school that didn't have a reputation for producing a lot of scholars. Our parents were mostly blue collar, who made it through the Great Depression and World War II. My own mother was a seamstress, and my father was a factory worker at Singer's Sewing Machines. Many of us were destined to follow in our fathers' footsteps.

My close friends were all locals who cared more about fast cars than anything else. Times were good, even with the war hanging over our heads. As I recall, not many of us knew much about what was going on in Southeast Asia, nor did we care. Once everyone and their brother was being drafted, we were forced to make decisions that defined our lives. This book recounts a period from spring 1966, when I was a senior in high school, through summer 1969, when my days of being a sailor ended. As high school wound down, all the buzz around school was what we were all going to do once we graduated.

While we had all heard bits and pieces about Vietnam, none of us knew much about this war 10,000 miles away. Everyone was talking about the plans they had: go to college, start working, or wait to get drafted and see what happened next.

I had thought about what I was going to do after high school for a long time. College was out of the question, as I wasn't exactly college material at the time.

My Uncle, a Naval Sailor that served in World War II, was my impetus to join the navy. Because I had always looked up to him growing up, it was an easy decision to make: the Draft heavily favored the Army, and I wasn't about to take my chances in a Fox Hole, that was for sure.

One night in my senior year, my dad and I were discussing what I was planning on doing after high school. As I was only 17, I needed his authorization to join the Navy. When I told him I was going to join the service after graduation, my father, an Army veteran who had served in World War II, said, "I will not sign for you if you are going into the Army."

I told him I was really interested in being a Sailor. "That's a great choice," he said with relief. "Three squares[1] a day, and a dry place to sleep." Later, I would hear my mom speaking to him, fearful of this upcoming change for me. I still remember my father, calmly saying to her, "It'll make a man out of him. He will be okay."

---

[1] square meals

One visit to the recruiting office later, and I had signed up to be inducted and start Active Duty the first week of September, 1966.

My friends and I finished high school, said goodbye, and went our separate ways. Most of the fellas I went to high school with, I never saw again. Sadly, some of them got drafted, went overseas, and returned in body bags.

2

Boot Camp
June 1966

Before my reporting date, there was a formal swearing in ceremony in Newark, NJ. You may not be on active duty after this ceremony, but you're definitely committed to serve.

This ceremony was my first experience with "need-to-know." Afterward the ceremony, we were waiting in line and an officer was picking men out of the line (I thought randomly). When the man next to me was picked out, I asked someone nearby, "What was that about?"

"They're Marines now," he said. For a minute, I thought that that could have been me.

Summer vacation that year flew by in a flash. No work for me: I was getting myself prepped to go into the US Navy and September 8th couldn't come soon enough.

I still remember that it was a Thursday. Early in the morning, I was escorted by my parents to Fort Hamilton in Brooklyn, New York, to start my military career.

As I left that morning, my brother said to me, "Good luck. Don't take any shit from anyone."

I remember arriving at Fort Hamilton. We said our goodbyes, and off I went. All recruits were corralled into a waiting room, given instructions, and told to just stay put.

That afternoon, we boarded a train bound for Chicago, one of my first of many overnight adventures to come. Around 9 a.m. Friday morning, we pulled into Chicago. From there, we were shuttled to Great Lakes Training Center for Navy recruits.

Now at this point, we were no longer civilians, but in transition to become sailors. The first weekend we spent in some old run-down, dingy barracks. *Is this what I signed up for?* I thought.

As it happened, this was a temporary situation for us, as bright and early Monday morning we were marched over to what was to be our living quarters for the next 10 weeks. "Not bad," I realized, as at least these buildings were fairly new.

Basic Training is a daily adventure in learning the ropes. Call it training, indoctrination, or brainwashing: you were there to learn how to follow the rules. I recall receiving my first sea bag of Navy issue clothing. "Go try these on," the sailor behind the counter barked at me. Well, the blue jeans fit, but nothing else.

I timidly went back and told him that my dress blue uniform was way too tight and didn't fit. One look at me, and he replied, "By the time you need to put those on, they will. Keep going."

What did I get myself into? The very next day we started our formal training.

As I remember it, it was a pep talk of sorts. The lecturer started by saying , "You guys are all wondering how you are going to get through this. Well, here's how: keep your mouth shut and do what you are told, and you won't have any problems.

Just what I needed: a way to get through this mess I had gotten myself into.

Week after week after week of marching, classroom orientation, drills, more marching, calisthenics, more classroom stuff, and we were half way there.

Then, a break to the mess decks for a week or so. Half of our company was the day shift working in the galley[2], while the other half was ordered to the night shift doing prep work for the following days meals.

My particular job the first night was to peel potatoes for 10,000 recruits. I was ushered into a big room with ancient appliances that looked somewhat like washing machines. They had an open top, into which you poured the potatoes. After a five-minute course on the care and operation of these antiques, I was left to my work (and more potatoes than I had ever seen in my life).

Once the machine started spinning and shooting water around the barrel, a wheelabrating method got off most of the skins. There were six machines with shoots that emptied into a large bin

---

[2] Kitchen

filled with water. After several minutes of spinning a trap door was opened and the potatoes emptied into the bin.

The job wasn't complicated, but it was all I could do to keep all machines running at once. After skinning an untold amount of 50-lb potato bags, I was finally done.

That really wasn't too bad, I thought. I proceeded out into the prep room to go back to the barracks and get some sleep.

The guy in charge had other ideas.

"Here's a peeler," he said, "finish taking off all of the skins that the machine didn't get."

That went on for a few nights, and I finally got the hang of the job. After the third night, those potatoes didn't have any skins on them... though I may have cut them a little deep.

Our next job on mess decks duty was cooking doughnuts, which was mostly an automated process. We made thousands of them each evening, in *Plain* and *Special* (sugar coated).

Just like Axel Grease Tony's doughnut shop back home, I thought.

Back in Elizabeth, Tony had an old truck that he converted into a doughnut factory, back before food trucks were a national phenomenon. Every day, he would drive his truck to the same place, crank up the doughnut making machine and sell them all day long for 40¢ / dozen. *Plain* and *Special* was all he had, too!

When mess cooking finally came to an end, it was back to more marching, drilling and learning about the Navy. Then, finally we were ready to graduate and go out into the fleet.

After nine weeks of waiting and wondering if my dress blues would fit, I tried them on. It was a miracle: I must've dropped 20 pounds! I felt good.

While we waited for our orders, everyone wondered where they would wind up. About a week before departing, all orders were listed on the bulletin board. I had requested East Coast duty, and felt fortunate that I got what I asked for.

I had been assigned to the *USS Douglas H. Fox DD-779*, home port of Norfolk, Virginia, one of the biggest Naval bases in the country. *Not too far from home,* I thought.

Hours after graduation, everyone departed for two weeks of leave before reporting to their first duty station.

3

USS Douglas H. Fox
December 1966

After a much-needed two-week leave at home, I was ready to join the fleet. Upon reporting to the Norfolk Naval Shipyard the second week of December, 1966, I was informed that the *Fox* was returning from a seven-month deployment in the Mediterranean Sea, and wouldn't be back in home port for another week.

I spent a week at the base barracks anxiously awaiting my ship to come in so I could start being a real sailor. On December 17th, I got notice that the *Fox* was coming into port, so I packed my sea bag and mustered down to the piers to report for duty.

I stood on the pier and watched my new home pull into port. I felt electric: I was finally going to get a taste of real Navy life! Of course, there were many other new recruits, just as green as I was, waiting to board a Navy vessel for the first time. As more than half the crew disembarked from the ship, we all wondered what was in store for us, and we soon found out.

As we ascended the gangplank and boarded the ship, the master-at-arms was there to take us to our quarters. The ship was like a ghost town, as many of the sailors had already departed on leave. We descended the ladder below-decks, wide-eyed at the exposed network of pipes and electrical wires. To that point, most of the ship's operations were still foreign to me.

We were ushered to our berthing compartments and assigned to our racks. *Pretty spartan accommodations,* I thought. This was 1st Division, better known as the Deck Force, or Boatswain Mates' Division. I was finally a sailor.

The *Fox* was a World War II Destroyer (a tin can, informally), and she was starting to show her age, especially after a seven month cruise in the Mediterranean Sea. The racks were three-high, and as a new recruit I got the bottom bunk. My locker barely fit all of my sea bag. *Guess I'll just have to make do,* I thought.

The bottom bunk sits directly over the lockers, and when sailors come back from liberty, they have to store their belongings. If they get back late and you are sleeping in the bottom bunk? Tough: get out of your rack so the guy can store his stuff.

A couple days after settling in, I reported to the mess decks for 12 weeks of what they called a *Tour of Additional Duty* (T.A.D.). Mess cooking normally fell upon the new recruits, so every division on the ship sent one or two guys on a rotating basis to the mess decks.

Our jobs varied, but basically we cleaned, cleaned, and cleaned some more. When we weren't wiping down tables or swabbing decks, we were washing pots and scrubbing out the cauldron used for cooking. We peeled potatoes in the spud locker (really, just more cleaning), and prepared salads too. During mealtimes, we worked in the scullery washing the crew's dishes.

The galley where the food was prepared was on one deck, while the actual mess deck where the enlisted men ate was one deck below. Bringing the food down the narrow ladder was tricky, but we got the hang of it.

Luckily, all of my mess deck duties took place while we were in port. I could never imagine what moving food from one level to another while underway would have been like!

Hours were long, and time off short. 12-hour days (or more) were typical. After three months of this, I was finally relieved of mess cooking duties and back in 1st Division, where I became a boatswain's mate, or deck hand. The guy who relieved me on the T.A.D. (I'll call him Dennis) was from 1st Division too, and was having a lot of trouble fitting in. We became friends, and often discussed our new lives as sailors. For sure, I was having a far easier time with this new lifestyle than he was.

Painting was a continual chore but not without its own fun. While in port, we did the sides of the ship. I recall once, I was on deck tending the lines and sending down paint for the sailor on the scaffolding. The chief boatswain's mate came by to check the progress on this paint job, and caught the seaman down below napping on the job! Gesturing everyone to be quiet, he took the 3rd Class Boatswain's mate's knife. The chief promptly cut the line and the sailor fell into the water! The sailor surfaced to the chief barking at him, "Don't ever let me catch you sleeping on the job again!"

After three months in Norfolk getting the ship ready to sail, we finally left port sometime in March for the Caribbean, with a stop in Miami. Being out at sea for the first time was quite an adventure (I never knew I was prone to motion sickness).

I'll never forget the day that we finally pulled into Miami. Lawrence was with me in 1st Division, and came aboard the same time I did. A big black guy from the south, he joined me in Miami the first day.

We stopped at a café in town for something to eat, but a sign on the door read **"No Coloreds Allowed."** I had never experienced anything like this before, and was shocked at the sight. Lawrence, on the other hand, just shrugged his shoulders. "Let's find another place to eat," was all he said. He didn't want to make a big deal of it, but I had never seen something like that where I grew up. My first port of call and I was already learning how different other parts of the world were, and we hadn't even left American shores yet! It was a very different country for anyone that looked like Lawrence.

After a few days of liberty, we were back out at sea doing maneuvers[3]. Even in 1967, our ship had remotely piloted drones on board, and back then, they weren't cheap! During one of the exercises, one of the drones went down in the ocean, never to be seen again. I know some officer caught hell for that debacle.

---

[3] A ship stationed in a no-combat zone, running normal duties with a crew of various levels of experience, so that when the ship is dispatched to a combat zone, there are no surprises.

Dennis continued to hate the Navy. One day during our daily nooner, while everyone was relaxing and taking in the sunshine on the fantail, Dennis calmly walked aft and took his clothes off. A couple of sailors asked him what he was doing.

"I'm going for a swim!" He called as he departed, diving over the lifeline and into the ocean wearing just his skivvies.

There was a mad scramble as the aft look-out, shocked, relayed to the bridge: "Man overboard! Man overboard! This is not a drill!" Fortunately, we were operating with an aircraft carrier that sent a helicopter to pick poor Dennis up.

After retrieving him from the ocean, they flew over the bridge of the *Fox*, and I can still remember Dennis waving to the Captain! Later that day, he ordered Dennis's belongings sent to the carrier, and said that he never wanted him back on his ship. A few months later, I heard that he got a medical discharge. I often wonder what ever happened to him.

Once we were back in Norfolk, it was business as usual on the *Fox*. This time, we were moored three or four ships out from the dock, so each exit from the ship involved passing through the other ships' quarterdecks to get dock-side. Moored at the pier was a ship called the *USS DuPont*. While still a tin can, she was much sleeker, longer and much more modern than the World War II rust bucket I was assigned to. I had heard a little bit about this ship from time to time. Unlike the Fox, her berthing quarters were air conditioned! I silently wondered what it would be like to serve on this ship.

The scuttlebutt around the *Fox* was that we were getting ready to take another Mediterranean cruise in a few months time. That didn't seem so terrible: I had never been overseas!

A month or so later, we were still in port. There was a notice in the plan of the day that the *DuPont* was being deployed to Vietnam in June, looking to fill some open spots. A clean start as a seaman on a new ship seemed like a good option for me, so I promptly put in a request for duty on the *DuPont*. In June 1967 I was re-assigned to the *USS DuPont DD-941*.

4

USS DuPont DD-941
June 1967

The last week or so on the *Fox,* it was difficult containing my excitement for my pending transfer. There was my new home, several berths away, just waiting for me to come aboard!

I mustered up the gang plank onto the *DuPont* with my sea bag in tow on a sunny day in June, 1967. The *DuPont* was all I hoped she would be. The current crew had been busy for the last three months getting her ready to deploy for Vietnam. Compared to the vintage tin can I had just left a moment ago, she looked brand new! The passageways were clean, with bright linoleum decks. The bulkheads shined with fresh paint. The mess decks were all on one level!

Descending, I noticed that even the ladders seemed wider. Our berthing compartment, though it housed at least 35 sailors, was much larger than those on the *Fox*, and it was air-conditioned! Any doubts I had before about moving to a new ship quickly dissipated: this comfort alone was worth the switch. Many of the sailors who had gotten her ready for the coming voyage were called short-timers and weren't joining us. This left a bunch of openings for the rest of the new crew and myself. I was given a middle bunk, and a much larger foot locker than I was used to. *Quite a change,* I thought.

I quickly settled into my new environment and began to get to know my new shipmates. There was a versatile mix of seasoned sailors (called *lifers*), combined with a much younger group of eager seamen like myself. *This is going to work out fine,* I thought.

Most guys get thrown into 1st division as their first ship assignment. Some would stay in the division and become boatswain mates, while others would hold out for an opening and transfer into a new division / rate. The rest of us? We just did our time and stayed put. At this point, I was just glad to be starting a new adventure on a different ship. It didn't really matter to me what I did on board.

We left Norfolk around June 20th, 1967, and headed straight for the Panama Canal. At the time I was pulling in about $85 every two weeks, without any expenses for room & board. Not bad for my first job after high school!

That week, we received our first pay. While in line to collect, I noticed two sailors at the end of the line collecting money from several sailors after they had received their stipend. Turning to the guy behind me, I asked what they were doing. "Oh, they run a slush fund," he answered. I needed more intel, but this wasn't the time or the place to get it.

I sought more information after returning to my duty station, and quickly got a lesson in finance from one of the other enlisted men.

16

"Sometimes sailors run out of money between pay days, and need to borrow. Several guys lend out cash until the next pay day comes around - usually $10 for $14 later, sometimes higher overseas. Many of these guys don't care about the interest. When pay day comes, we are often out to sea and they don't need cash for anything anyway."

"How do I get involved in this?"

"Just pass the word around your division that you have money to lend. The word will spread."

As I started to put the pieces together for my new side business, I asked, "What happens if they don't pay me back?"

"Then they get black-listed and no one loans them anything. It all works out fine the majority of the time. Just keep a low profile and good records." That was all I needed to get rolling.

About a week or so after leaving Norfolk, we were scheduled to pull into Rodman Naval Station in the Panama Canal Zone. Today, Rodman Naval Station is operated by the Panamanian government, but in 1967, this was a US Navy Station.

I had read about this place growing up, but admittedly, I really didn't know much about it or the crossing from the Atlantic to the Pacific through the Canal. For many of the seaman aboard, like myself, this was our first transit and we looked forward to the experience.

The day before pulling into the Canal, the Captain gave us some details. "After we complete our transit through the canal we will be in Gatun Lake. This is a fresh water lake, and it will be the first time *The DuPont* will be in fresh water since it was commissioned over ten years ago. The crew will be manning all hoses about the ship for a thorough cleaning."

Scattered about the ship, there were numerous high-powered hoses on the main decks. These were to be used in case of emergencies to control fires aboard a ship. The engineering divisions were responsible for fitting every hose aboard the ship to pump water in from the lake.

Once the hoses were set, every division that had a working space outside on the main decks was involved in the "working party." As it happened, 1st Division was responsible for most everything outside the skin of the ship.

We were warned beforehand that these hoses were high-pressure, and if we were not careful, someone could wind up in sick bay. I had never power-washed anything before, so this turned out to be quite a treat. Like washing your car, if your car was 500 feet long.

All outside hatches were secured before activating the hoses. After this was done, the hoses were pressurized and we had the task of washing all outside bulkheads, ladders and decks on every level of the ship. Our division's sailors were all over the main decks, manning the hoses. It took us a couple of hours to complete, but it was more fun than work.

The next day, we were in the Pacific Ocean, and on our way to San Diego.

5

En route to West Pac via San Diego
June 1967

As we steamed north for San Diego, the weather was great, and the ocean was a sheet of glass. Fifty years may be coloring my memory, but I recall the Pacific Ocean looking much bluer than the Atlantic.

A couple days out to sea, I was put in charge of the 1st Division paint locker. Here I was, an eighteen-year-old seaman, in charge of something! I thought that this was the greatest thing that could happen to me.

After a couple weeks, I realized that this was probably the worst job on the ship, right down there with mess cooking. The man in charge of the paint locker handed out paint brushes & rollers to everyone in the morning, and cleaned them twice a day. Cleaning involved a soak in diesel fuel, which had to be obtained below-decks, which was hand-carried in a five-gallon can up two decks to the paint locker.

I also had to keep track of inventory. The excess paint that wouldn't fit into the paint locker was stored forward, in the bosun locker. Luckily, I had assistance in hauling the paint out of the hole it was in.

After a couple of weeks, I figured out that we had enough brushes and rollers aboard to supply the whole fleet. It was easier to hand out new brushes instead of cleaning them every day, so used ones on this cruise mostly wound up in Davy Jones' Locker. Since I had to request new ones from the Supply Division, a young supply officer commented to me more than once, "You guys sure use a lot of paint brushes."

"Well, we want the ship to look good for the Captain, don't we?" Nobody asked any questions after that.

A couple days from San Diego, we got word that additional sailors would be joining our crew once we pulled into port. To my surprise, one of the guys to come on board was a former high school classmate of mine!

Greg had graduated the same year as I did. We joined the Navy around the same time, but after boot camp he qualified for "A School" and had spent the past 6 months training to be a Yeoman (ships' office duties). There were no openings in the ship's office at present, so Greg was remanded to 1st Division until there was an opening.

Having a shipmate on board from my hometown was a real bonus for the both of us and we fast became close friends. *The DuPont* spent a few days in San Diego for Independence Day, and we took on supplies, food, and fuel before heading for Hawaii.

6

Hawaii & Midway Island
July 1967

The DuPont left San Diego on schedule and steamed west for about a week before pulling into Pearl Harbor, with smooth sailing the whole time. The crew was now into a daily routine of shipboard duties and standing watches.

Each division had a certain responsibility for making sure the ship ran smoothly. Ours was structured into four sections, giving us four hours on watch and eight hours off.

I came to realize very quickly that this meant only one full night's sleep every four days. When not on watch it was our division's responsibility to keep the ship looking brand new. That included cleaning and painting anything that didn't move. If it moved, we made sure it was tied down.

After we finished painting a bulkhead or a deck, a week later we did it again. *No wonder we used up so much paint!* I thought. Maintaining the cleanliness and care of the ship was a never-ending chore. If you've ever heard "ship-shape," this is where it comes from.

When we were not keeping the ship sparkling, we were on watch. 1st Division's responsibilities included bridge watches, lookout watches, after steering and after lookout watch.

In addition to serving as lookouts, we were responsible for maintaining the ship's speed (Lee-Helm) and staying on course (Helm). After about twenty minutes of learning how to steer the ship, you were on your own. I guess they figured you couldn't hit much in the middle of the ocean, so it was pretty safe.

After Steering was in a small compartment below-decks. It had a helm (steering wheel), and a compass for navigation purposes as well. If we somehow lost steering up on the bridge, After Steering would take over navigation using the compass.

Occasionally, the bridge would switch to After Steering to ensure that everything was in working order, but we got relieved from the bridge every couple of hours.

Being assigned After Steering watch was great! You put your sound-powered headphones[1] on, and if you were needed, they would phone you. All we had to do was hang out, and even sleep if we wanted to! Also great: we generally knew ahead of time if there was going to be a drill, thanks to the previous watch that would give us the heads up.

After lookout was just that: look aft. Keep an eye on everything behind the ship. Easy job. Some guys would rather be on the

---

[1] Sound-powered headphones are a special shipboard communication tool that allows two locations to transmit audio, even in the absence of ship's power.

bridge, hanging out with the crew and chatting with the officers, but I thought the After Lookout Watch was a great assignment. Alone at the aft end of the ship, you could even smoke if you wanted. No smoking on the bridge (unless you were the Captain: he could do whatever he wanted).

We got to know the officers on Bridge Watch, but we had to be on our best behavior. Proper protocol prevailed at all times while on the bridge.

Mid watch (12-4 AM) was the worst. Getting up at 11:30 pm to stand four hours on a dark bridge was my least favorite thing to do on board, and incidentally, where I learned to sleep standing up.

As we pulled into Pearl Harbor, we couldn't help but think about the surprise attack that pulled the USA into the Pacific Front of WWII and changed the course of the war. Many of us weren't even born then, so we could only imagine what it was like that day.

As a major part of US history, it was eerie sailing through the harbor and past the memorial to the USS Arizona. Many of the ship's crew took the trip out and toured this monument, but while the *DuPont* pulled into Pearl several times during our two West Pac cruises, touring the memorial was too much for me to bear during any of our visits.

❖ ❖

That said, it was really a treat visiting Honolulu, and seeing all the sights was great. It was the middle of July, but little did I know what was going on back in my home-town five thousand miles away.

Passing by a newsstand, I noticed a headline in one of the local newspapers: *"Newark under siege!"* Elizabeth was a mere six miles away from Newark! Out at sea, we had no idea of the turmoil back in the states. Race riots were happening in many of the big cities across the USA.

Picking a time when I knew everyone at home would be available, I called to get the details. I figured things had to be pretty bad if Newark, New Jersey was making headlines in Hawaii. My family assured me that the rioting wasn't nearly as bad in Elizabeth as it was in Newark, but everyone was told to stay indoors until things blew over.

Relieved, I told my family about where the ship was, and what we were up to. Up until this point I don't think they knew much about where the ship was headed, or what we were going to do once we got to our destination. The war wasn't going to impact the DuPont for another month. After taking on more food and fuel, it was time to set sail again for the Western Pacific Ocean.

Fortunately, we did not experience any serious racial tension on the *DuPont*. Everyone on the ship had a job to do, and I never got the sense that anyone felt discriminated against.

On the way to the Philippines, we made a fueling stop at Mid-Way Island, home of the famous albatross, with a wing-span of up to twelve feet! At the time, everyone called them Gooney Birds. I had never heard of this species before.

As we were pulling into port, we caught our first glimpse of them in flight. Swooping down to snag a fish, the Gooney bird hit the water and did a tumbling act for us, rather than pick the fish out of the water. What a sight to see.

They didn't do much better flying into trees. Rather than landing carefully on an extended branch, these birds would fly directly into the tree: not something I would soon forget.

After a quick refueling stop, we were off again. Next stop would be Subic Bay, in the Philippines.

7

Subic Bay, Olongapo City, The Philippines
July 1967

Except for a quick stop in the Panama Canal, Subic Bay would be, for many of us, our first visit to a foreign port. About a day before getting into Subic Bay, our department officer briefed us on the city we were about to visit. He gave us some pointers on what to do (and more importantly, what not to do).

"First of all," he told us, "never go into town alone. Always be with at least one shipmate. If you see any US Marines, don't mess with them. However," he paused, looking around the room. "If you get into trouble in town, or in one of the local bars, THEN seek out a Marine. They will always help you."

Some of these foreign ports were dangerous, so knowing who we could rely on for help when needed was reassuring. Some of my shipmates called on the Marines more than once for help on our cruise.

Subic Bay was one of the biggest, and one of the most important, US Naval Bases west of Pearl Harbor. A repair base as well, the vast majority of US ships operating off the coast of

Vietnam made frequent stops at Subic Bay on the way to and from the gun line[1].

We pulled into Subic Bay the same day as the *USS Forrestal*, an aircraft carrier that caught fire out at sea. She limped into port two days after the accident, listing[2] and still smoking from the fire that had caused so much carnage.

A couple of us were at the Enlisted Mans Club[3] having a drink before heading into town when a few seaman from the *Forrestal* came in and joined us. They looked haggard and exhausted. They told us it had been a couple days since they had slept, but most anyone who was able got a liberty pass for some well-deserved time off the ship.

We were treated to a couple horror stories, which made us *DuPont* sailors realize how fortunate we were to be on a tin can. Small ships usually equal small problems, but ships don't get bigger than aircraft carriers (a big ship equals big problems).

◆ ◆

Nothing will ever compare to the stench of Olongapo. As we went through the main gate, to enter the city we crossed a bridge over a body of "water" that I learned was known as the *shit river*.

---

[1] When a ship is in artillery firing range, they are on the gun line.

[2] leaning to one side.

[3] an on-base bar for enlisted men like myself.

28

Off to one side was a row of houses (shacks, really), that had railings over the river, which served as their toilet. This in itself was bad enough, but on the bridge were local kids, not much more than 10 or 12 years old, who dove into the river when sailors threw money into the water. Looking back, I can see how nothing had prepared us for this situation, and how easy it was to just join in on the "fun." Before this moment, I had never realized how good I had it growing up. We were eighteen-year-old kids, seeing third-world poverty for the first time, and it didn't quite feel real. Looking back, throwing money into the *shit river* would not be any of our prouder moments.

This town was nothing like anything I had ever seen before. It was block after block of bars, restaurants and souvenir shops as far as the eye could see. Old converted jeeps shuttled sailors and locals alike to their destinations. We soon learned that you could get anything you wanted in Olongapo.

Not having eaten before leaving our ship, we figured we would grab something to eat in town, at one of the many push carts along the city streets. *Meat-on-a-stick* seemed to be the favorite of the locals. *When in Rome* I thought, and ordered one.

After a couple of bites that seemed a little too spicy for my palate, I asked what it was I was eating. "That's monkey meat, *Sailor Joe,*"[4] came the reply. After spitting it out, I asked if he had anything else I could try. "Yes," he said, "I have dog over here,"

---

[4] A common nickname for seamen in the Pacific

pointing to some sticks on the other side of the cart. I politely declined the dog and wound up drinking my dinner that night.

We were scheduled to be in port for about eight days, before heading to the gun line. During that time I realized that a lot of my shipmates had no idea how to budget their meager earnings. After the fourth day in port, my slush fund program was starting to get some activity. Loan someone ten bucks and in two weeks you get fourteen? Even with my limited math skills I realized that this was going to be a very profitable venture.

Liberty at the China Sea Club in Subic Bay

Over the next year and a half the *DuPont* would return several times to this great liberty port.

We spent the last couple days getting ready for our initial stint on the gun line. After bringing on sufficient amount of food, ammo and topping off our fuel tanks, it was time to hit the gun line and do some damage.

8

Gun Line
August 1967

It took us a mere two days of steaming to reach the gun line off the coast of Vietnam. *Preparation* and *readiness* were the words we heard most often during this transit from the Philippines to the Gulf of Tonkin. The vast majority of us had never been in combat and had no idea what we were about to experience.

The first major change of our daily routine at the gun line was being adjusted to *Port and Starboard Watch*, a fancy name for six hours on and six hours off, around the clock. So while half of the crew stood watch and manned their stations, the other half rested.

The four departments on board – Operations, Engineering, Weapons, and Supply – all had their defined duties. Each department officer had the responsibility of keeping his department running like a clock without missing a single tick. No one on board was exempt; even the cooks had to make sure the ship was well fed during these operations.

1st division was part of the weapons department, evenly split up into two sections. The watches changed hands at 6 a.m., noon, 6 p.m., and midnight. This schedule mostly allowed ample time for everyone to have an uninterrupted meal. Attached to the weapons department, our functions were to man the bridge watches, After Steering, lookout, and handling ammo in the magazines. Six-on, six-off wasn't so bad.

After a couple weeks we were pretty much into our new routine, firing at the enemy from several miles off of the coast, well out of harm's way.[1]

During the 30 days between Norfolk and the gun line, the *DuPont* held many simulations to prepare us for our upcoming missions off the coast of Vietnam. We were called to General Quarters more than once during these trial runs for the crew.

General Quarters is an all-hands-on-deck situation, where everyone has an assignment; my duty station during General Quarters was on the bridge. It was common for these drills to take place at the most inopportune moments (dinner, 2 AM, etc). While necessary to test the readiness of the crew, drills never really prepare you for the real thing.

The old salts on board couldn't stress enough that we were going into a war zone, in support of US troops inland in Vietnam. The majority of our crew had never been in a war zone before this deployment. A lot of us were barely out of high school, not yet 20 years old. This was all new territory to us.

---

[1] The DuPont had three gun mounts: one forward and two aft, with a maximum firing capacity of about 40 rounds per minute if all systems were working optimally.

Several times, the DuPont was taken under fire. We had been operating on the gun line since August 7th. For the first couple of weeks things were fairly routine. Port and Starboard watches were going smoothly. Having both bridge and magazine duty broke up the monotony somewhat.

On August 28th, while on-station, we got a message that one of the ships we were operating with, the USS Robison DDG-12, was being fired upon, and coming to her aid painted a target on us as well. On this particular day, I was in the forward magazine feeding rounds of ammo to Mount 51. Our job was to keep the gun mount above us filled with ammo.

Up until this point things had been fairly calm. Suddenly we got a message from the gunner's mate in mount 51 that we had just taken a direct hit.

There was a look of surprise and shock from my fellow shipmates in the magazine when we were told we just took a hit at one of the gun mounts aft. I never felt that we were in imminent danger, but the realization that we were at war was finally sinking in. I remember being a little nervous. This was the real thing. We had been prepped for this for over a month, but it still shook us up.

"Start loading ammo and don't stop until I tell you to," I remember hearing.

General Quarters was called, and all hands reported to their duty stations. Once all hands were called and teams had time to get into position, the sailors in charge of each duty station would report all personnel accounted for or missing.

34

As I was on my way to my station, my path took me through the mess decks. Oh my way, two fellow sailors came through carrying a man on a stretcher. I later learned that it was Frank Bellant, a fireman in the engineering department. When we took a hit, he was right below the explosion.

Frank was our only fatality on the gunline. There were also eight men injured from the same shot, hitting us directly on an aft gun mount. This was not what I had expected during this deployment.

Aftermath of the hit on our aft mount.

To this day, I am sure that everyone on board the DuPont that day remembers where they were when we were hit.

With one mount out of commission, we still had two others which were in fine working order. So, we were able to stay on the gun line for another two weeks before heading back to Subic Bay for much needed repairs.

❖❖

When not on patrol, we were somewhere in the Pacific, taking on more ammo, food or fuel. We called these underway replenishments "unreps", done out at sea while cruising at 15 knots or so.

Two ships performing unreps (the DuPont *is next in line)*

Unrepping was quite a sight to see. We would pull alongside a replenishment ship, maintain the exact speed they were at and start the process of transferring whatever we needed.

36

For food and ammo, this was an all-hands-on-deck chore: no one except the engine room personnel and bridge watches were exempt. The crew made a chain from amidships[2] (where the goods came aboard) to wherever goods were headed. Very time consuming.

We re-fueled at night on more than one occasion. While this wasn't an all-hands-on-deck unrep, it wasn't nearly as safe.

If you were off duty when it was time for replenishments, tough luck: you missed your sleep. More than once, there were replenishments several nights in a row, and nobody got any sleep.

As September 12th approached, we were all ready to head to port for some liberty. We had been out to sea for over 30 days by the time our first stint on the gun line was over. Subic Bay never looked so good.

---

[2] The middle of the ship.

Interlude

Family Gram #3, September 1967

    CDR R. H. Small, USN, Commanding Officer USS DuPont (DD941)

The past month and a half since my last letter to you has been the most important period that DuPont has experienced since commissioning. It has been filled with pride in many jobs well done, sorry from the death of a shipmate, many long hours and hard work, and the knowledge of knowing we have measurably helped our fellow countrymen and allies in keeping south Vietnam free.

As I write this we are again tied up in Subic Bay, Republic of the Philippines for our scheduled "availability" for repairs, rest, and recreation. Just outboard of us is the Australian Navy Guided Missile destroyer HMAS Perth (D-38). *She is a fine example of that country's naval support in the struggle for Vietnam. We expect to share the Gunline with her sometime during our next cruise as we did with her sister ship the* HMAS Hobart (D-39). *The weather since we've been here has improved considerably over our last visit and we have found that he sun does actually shine now and then.*

On 5 August DuPont got underway from this port and headed for Danang, South Vietnam. There we relieved the destroyer USS Morton (DD 948). *Commodore Cornwall,* Comdesron 22, *Relieved* Comdesdiv 92 *as commander of all the gunfire support ships stations off the coast of South Vietnam. After briefings were completed, DuPont weighed anchor and headed north to the Demilitarized Zone (known as the DMZ) between North and South Vietnam. There we began providing gunfire support for the 12th Marine Regiment. The job was a hard one. We basically split the officers and crew into two sections, port and starboard, and fired our guns around the clock. Each section had 6 hours of duty followed by 6 hours off. After 34 days of this it almost became a habit. And it was surprising how quickly we all became used to sleeping through the noise of gunfire. By the time we arrived her in Subic we had actually worn out all our 5 inch gun barrels and fired more than 8500 rounds.*

It is almost impossible to list all DuPont's accomplishments during this past month so I have enclosed excerpts from the daily statements released to the press in Saigon. These give some idea of the job DuPont has been doing over here. But all these results have not been without cost. On the 28th while trying to silence some artillery pieces which were shelling U.S. Marines, we and the USS Robison (DDG-12) *were taken under heavy fire by North Vietnamese coastal batteries. Although we were able to return the fire and avoid most of the rounds fired at us, one struck the barrel of Mount 52. Shrapnel from the blast penetrated into the ship killing Fireman Frank L. Bellant. It also wounded seven other men. The entire crew was shocked and saddened by Frank's death but in spite of this they all continued to do an outstanding job, and the ship returned to the gunline to continue firing at the enemy.*

To set your minds at ease I will list the names of our casualties. Only two, Russell Rader and John Layne, required hospitalization and they were taken by helicopter to the USS Tripoli (LPH-10). *All the others were returned to duty the same day after treatment in our Sick Bay. Russell Radar is on his way back to the ship at this time.*

Killed in Action:

Frank L. Bellant, Flint Michigan

Wounded in Action

John R. Layne, Russell P. Rader, James P. Abrashinsky, James M. Doll, Joseph A. Griffin, Wayne Miller, and James C Young.

Since we have been underway this past month we have received word of the birth of twin girls to Radarman Second Class and Mrs. Samuel C. Hammett, Jr. and a baby boy to Sonar Technician Third Class and Mrs. David W. Gerwin. We have also promoted the following men: Larnzie T. Porter to SD3, William W. Day to SK3, Vernon G. Hall to EN3, Frank Lott to EN3, Frank P. McDonough to MM3, William E. Campion to ETN 3, Donald R. Kuemerle to EM3, Jeffery A. Seeley to YN3, Ralph L. Petty to GMG3, Joseph Richardson to ETN3, James L. Black to TM3, and Carl J. Lewis to YN3.

After leaving Subic the end of this month we expect our schedule to be a little less demanding and are looking forward to visits to Manilla, Hong Kong, possibly Sasebo and Yokosuka, Japan. Our return to Norfolk, Virginia is still listed as 17 January 1968.

With the cruise nearly half over I am convinced that one of the biggest morale boosters is the letters we receive from home. Mail call is eagerly awaited by everyone. Some of the men only get bills and circulars but even these are read and reread. So please keep the mailman busy.

Best regards,

R.H. Small

9

Liberty Call
September 1967

The crew couldn't wait to get back to Subic Bay. After being out at sea for over 30 days, everyone was ready for some liberty, and this stretch in port turned out to be longer than expected due to the repairs the *DuPont* required. The local teams worked every day, and often into the evening, repairing the gun mount. This was all to get us ready to return to the gun line. It took a full two weeks to get Mount 52 repaired and ready.

Two weeks in port! A lot of my fellow sailors really did not know how to pace themselves with the limited amount of money they were earning, so after several days, the requests to borrow money started coming. Ten dollars here, ten dollars there, and pretty soon I had a lot of receivables on the books. My slush fund was working.

The majority of guys needing quick cash didn't really care about how much they had to pay back, figuring that when pay day came, they would be out to sea and wouldn't have anything to spend their money on anyway. Back in San Diego and Hawaii I had heard that this would happen once we hit the foreign ports, so I had been squirreling my money away. It was starting to pay off.

One afternoon, I got called into officers' quarters by one of the officers I knew from bridge watches. Wondering what this was all about, I calmly knocked on the door of his stateroom. "Come in," he motioned to me. "Shut the door."

Oh crap. I am in some kind of trouble, I immediately thought.

"So, I hear that some of the sailors on board run a slush fund." My blood ran cold. Not sure where this was headed, I just looked at him, quiet and dumbfounded. I did not want to implicate myself, or rat on my shipmates.

"Well," he continued, "the officers on board understand that the guys who run these slush funds provide a very valuable service to their shipmates. It probably keeps theft down as well.

"So we turn our heads and let you guys help out the sailors when they need a quick loan." I was starting to relax at this point, but still didn't know why I was sitting in this officer's state room. Was I getting a lecture? A reprimand? Or is this some kind of praise? I soon found out.

"So, you lend out $10 to a shipmate and get $14 back in two weeks? That's a 40% profit you are making."

I wasn't great with math, but I did realize that I was making a nice profit. I still hadn't confessed to him my involvement, for fear of a reprimand.

He continued. "Do you ever run short of cash between paydays?"

The conversation was getting relaxed now. I asked him, "Why do you ask?"

"As officers, we can't be involved with this kind of stuff at all. However, there is nothing that says I can't help you out if you need an advance to help a fellow sailor.

"So how does this sound: I have extra cash. I will give you $100 when you need it and when payday comes around, you pay me back $120. We split the profits. Okay?"

Well, this sounded good to me, and I told him I would be in touch with him the next time I ran short. *That wasn't so bad after all,* I thought.

I used this banker more than a few times during the rest of our deployment. Just about every payday, after everything was up to date, I would take a stroll into officers' quarters and get squared away with my new partner. This all worked out well for everyone in the end.

❖❖

Our division had the responsibility of always making sure the ship looked it's best, so painting the ship from top to bottom regularly was our job. The sides of the ship had not been painted for some time now, so the Chief Boatswain Mate decided to have it done while we had a few extra days here in port. All of us were in a hurry to get this job done so we could commence with liberty, but this was no easy or quick task.

First, the peeling areas had to be chipped and ground down to a smooth surface, then primed with red lead paint as a rust preventative. After the primer dried, we put the final grey coat of paint on.

Everyone assigned the task of painting the side of the ship normally paid attention to detail. This particular day, being in such a hurry, we didn't allow the red lead paint to thoroughly dry before painting over it with grey paint. Well, the combination of red lead paint and battleship grey eventually dried, resulting in a beautiful pink destroyer.

As close as we were to the job, we did not notice at least one section of the ship was now pink. The Chief, inspecting our work from the pier, was not happy. In rushing to get to liberty faster, we lost the whole day and had to re-paint everything.

Being in port for this long was a blessing, and going on liberty was always an adventure. Luckily, there were plenty of MPs[3] always patrolling the downtown area to keep peace among the sailors.

With lots to see and do, everything was cheap in this port. But we had to be extra careful of the locals: some would rob you blind at the first chance they got. Sticking together, we were able to keep an eye out for each other.

---

[3] Military Police

Two weeks flew by in a flash, but it was probably enough time for the crew to rest up and prepare once again for the rigors of Port and Starboard Watch. The gun mount was 100% ready for more fire support off the Vietnam coast. Off we went, back to the gun line, as we wondered what was in store for us this time around.

Interlude

Comments on an East Coast Destroyer's Vietnam Tours - First Deployment

CDR R. H. Small, USN, Commanding Officer USS DuPont (DD941)

At scheduled intervals, ships were relieved to proceed to ports outside the war zone for repairs and relaxation. Such places as Kaoshiung, Formosa, Subic Bay, P.I., Manilla, and Hong Kong, BCC, were visited. (No repair work could be done in Hong Kong because of Red Chinese protests). Besides repairs for shell damage, considerable work was needs-d to fix ruptured pipes, platings, decks, and bulkheads, and to reinstall compartment lights and fixtures.

These structural failures were caused by the continual shock of our own ship muzzle blasts. Undetected shock damage cracks in both emergency diesel generators exhaust piping resulted in a fire in the after part of the ship during the early hours of thee morning of 1 November while anchored in the harbor of Kaohsiung, Taiwan. Serious damage and disaster was prevented by exceptionally effective, well executed fire fighting by the ship's company.

10

Gun Line Round 2
Oct 1967

It took us a few days to get back to the gun line, reporting on a rotating basis with other tin cans. It was now their turn for R&R and our turn to patrol the coast.

We were always on high alert and complete readiness while off the coast, and our job was to maintain contact with the Army and Marines inland. They would provide us with coordinates and intel on what we were shooting at. The maximum accurate range for our 5" guns was around thirteen miles, well beyond the horizon. We normally operated about 5 miles or so off of the coast.

After receiving instructions we would move into position and fire one or two rounds, to see how close we were to our target. After several back and forth communications we would commence firing. After this engagement we would receive a damage report from the inland soldiers, if they were close enough to tell us what we hit. This went on day after day.

Every few days or so we would leave the coast for refueling, rearming or to take on supplies. It became pretty routine.

Many nights we were stationed in Da Nang Harbor, anchored very close to the shore. This was supposedly safe harbor for Navy ships, but we would often hear and see activity inland from the ship, as illuminating rounds lit up the sky. We could sometimes hear explosions in the distance.

One of the sailors from 1st Division had a brother who was a Marine, and patrolling in the immediate area. Our seaman put in a request with the Captain, asking if it would be possible for his brother to board the ship for a visit.

The Captain acknowledged immediately and gave permission to bring him aboard the *DuPont*. "We will get him a hot meal and a good night's sleep as well. Get him up to the bridge as soon as he comes aboard," the Captain said. I had bridge watch that night, so I would meet this Marine as well.

In a combat zone, lights are limited, and red on the bridge, but we got used to the dim conditions and could see fairly well during night watch. By the time he was brought aboard, it was dark aboard the *DuPont*.

When the Marine finally made it to the bridge, he met with the Captain briefly, and was introduced to the rest of the watch. I will never forget this exchange.

Though we were stationary, I was at the helm in case we had to get underway in a hurry. He came up to me, and we shook hands. He was big: so big, my 6' frame only made it to about his neck line.

Bathed in the dim red light of the bridge, it was then that I noticed a leather strap around his neck. On the end of the strap was a shriveled up ear. "My first gook," he said, noticing my stare.[4]

---

[4] During the Korean & Vietnam Wars, *gook* was frequently used as derogatory slang for a person from Southeast Asia.

11

Liberty: Hong Kong and Kaohsiung, Taiwan
Late October, 1967

After a few more weeks of gun line duties, this time without any major catastrophes, it was time for some more R&R, and a chance at some additional cash for my slush fund.

I thought I had seen it all in Subic Bay, but nothing quite prepared me for what was in store for us *DuPont* sailors in both Hong Kong and Kaohsiung. With no piers here to tie up against as in previous ports of call, we anchored out in the harbor and took a water taxi to & from the mainland. No ship repairs this time, just R&R.

Hong Kong was a major bustling city, with many different areas to explore. We had been warned about the dangers of traveling alone, so we all took the necessary precautions and always traveled with someone.

Custom tailors were abundant throughout the city, as were restaurants, and souvenir shops. With some extra funds available, I treated myself to a suit and a few bespoke shirts as well.

While heading back to our ship one evening, we ran into a street vendor selling Seiko watches for $5. What a great deal!

Proudly wearing my watch, I showed it to a seasoned sailor who had visited many overseas ports in his career. He said he was busy at the moment, but to come around tomorrow and show him my new watch. By the time I caught up with him the next day, it had stopped.

He just laughed, and asked me how much had that lesson cost me. After that I became very wary of anyone selling anything. A few days later, we were off to another port of call.

◆◆

Kaohsiung, Taiwan was controlled by mainland China, and the influence of the mother country was evident. Travel to port was via water taxi, which meant that anyone who had too much to drink in port had a rough time on the way back.

When we got to the pier there were plenty of different modes of transportation to get us where we were headed: I preferred the rickshaw, a small two-seater taxi on two wheels pulled by a man. Twenty-five cents took you wherever you wanted to go.

Like Subic Bay, Kaohsiung was full of bars, restaurants and souvenir shops, block after block. As usual, we were warned about traveling too far away from the main part of town, especially at night. The buddy system prevailed here for sure.

I still remember the food in Kaohsiung – lots of fried rice dishes, in big portions, for less than a taxi ride! They would serve it in a way I'd never seen before, too. The rice would be brought to your table on a plate, under a lid. Removing the lid, you'd see your rice in the exact shape of the lid, which had been filled up and packed tight. Incredible presentation.

Never in my life had I seen such a variety of things for sale. Swords, knives, statues, and knick-knacks of all kinds. Wood-carved Buddhas of all sizes by the hundreds. I loaded up on bootleg albums from bands I knew, a mere 25¢ each, compared to $2-3 at home.

The reverence for Chiang Kai-Shek, the military leader of mainland China, was clear. Nothing disparaging about this guy was spoken in Kaohsiung. His reputation, at least as far as we heard it, was that he could do no wrong.

Liberty often commenced early enough in the day that we had plenty of time to see the sites around town. Wandering the side streets was safe enough during the day.

A typical residential area was made up mostly of run-down shacks. I had already learned a lot in my first thirteen months in the Navy, but one thing continually reinforced for me at all these ports of call was how fortunate I was.

After four or five days of liberty here, money was starting to get a little scarce for some of my shipmates. I had been building up a cash reserve for my fellow sailors, and was prepared to help them out.

While sifting through some foreign change, I noticed that there was a National Taiwanese coin, identical in size to an American quarter, worth about 5¢ USD.

The soda machine on the *Dupont's* mess decks charged the crew 5¢ for a Coke. Imagine my reaction when I realized that I could use one of these coins to get a coke... and four nickels back as well! I was making 20 cents every time I drank a Coke! All I had to do was keep a supply of these quasi-quarters with me.

Hanging with shipmates at the Enlisted Man's Club

Of course, it didn't take long for the word to spread that there was a way to make money drinking soda. It didn't last long: after a few days, the machine ran out of nickels. When the supply officer opened the soda machine, he was pissed. There was a notice the next day to immediately cease & desist this thievery, and it was Captains Mast[1] for anyone caught doing that again. One warning was enough for us; it was fun while it lasted.

Our time in Kaohsiung came to an end on November 5th, and it was back to the gun line for one more rotation.

---

[1] Punishment that can range from reprimand, extra duty, reduction in rank, restrictions, or loss of pay.

12

Gun Line Round Three
November 1967

One more trip to the gun line, and we were done. The crew was well-prepared for this rotation, which was more of the same: coordinates from the Army & Marines inland, firing at targets, readjusting our aim, then letting loose with salvo after salvo of projectiles into the designated targets.

Bridge watches and magazine duty became routine for 1st Division. Our function down below was to make sure everything was ready when the call came to start loading.

Firing rounds was a two-step process. Prior to loading the ammo into the turnstile, each round had to have the cap removed and the round activated by turning a screw. Each turnstile held approximately 30 rounds, and a 5" projectile weighed about 40 pounds.

At the other side of the turnstile, the gunpowder was inserted. Each keg of gun powder weighed at least 40 pounds. Once prepped, the turnstile rotated the round and the gun powder into position. When the rounds were ready to be hoisted up, they went up hydraulically.

When we weren't firing and loading ammo, having magazine duty was the best: it was a place to rest and relax for a duty shift. However, sleeping on the job comes with an occupational hazard. Once, I was sleeping on top of a bunch of ammo in the magazine below Mount 51. The *DuPont* took an unexpected roll while changing course and a powder casing fell on my leg. The official log of the incident read, *"Tuesday Nov. 14, 1967 @ 1330 Perrotti, Raymond Joseph, B11-47-29 SA was struck with a powder case when it fell from the stack in MT 51 Magazine. In the line of duty. Diagnosis Bruise of the Lateral Left Thigh. Disposition: BED REST."* Maybe I should've gotten a Purple Heart for this? After all, I was injured in the line of duty in a war zone![1]

Our ship was designated as the command ship. As head of the squadron, we had the Commodore aboard. Unlike the Captain, who it seemed was always on the bridge, we rarely saw the Commodore. His presence aboard also meant that the *DuPont* got a lot of visitors.

While on bridge watch there were always swarms of officers and enlisted men coming and going with reports for the Captain. We often had personnel from other ships, and even officers from South Vietnam aboard too. The South Vietnamese military were seasoned and polished. They looked to me like they had smaller frames than their American counterparts. If we weren't on our

---

[1] No disrespect meant toward any of the brave soldiers and sailors who were injured *in combat* in a war zone.

best behavior, we would hear it from our division officer who would catch hell from the Captain.

At the end of this rotation, we were more than ready to head for home, but not before some additional liberty in another new foreign port.

Ready for liberty

Through three rotations on the gun line, the DuPont had some impressive stats. After 75 days of artillery support to our troops on land, we fired more than 20,000 rounds of ammo from our 5" guns. After over 2,000 fire missions, the DuPont was officially responsible for 136 structures destroyed, and 75 confirmed North Vietnamese killed.

All of this firing eventually took its toll on the *DuPont*. Throughout any area above the main deck of the ship, major wear & tear was evident to the super structure. Bulkheads, decks, lights and fixtures: all of it needed to be shown some care as the constant vibration of rounds of ammo being fired was finally beginning to show. However, none of this affected the integrity of the ship and its ability to run well. We finally left the gun line for the last time in early December, making a quick stop in Okinawa before heading into Yokosuka, Japan.

13

Leaving the Gun Line: Heading to Okinawa and Yokosuka
December 1967

In the first week of December, 1967, we headed North for Japan. Before heading into Yokosuka, our final foreign port, we made a quick stop in Okinawa, a beautiful island about 500 miles south of Japan in the East China Sea.

Several times while transiting the Pacific Ocean, we would get a history lesson from one of the officers about World War II, and the island we were about to visit, just as we did while approaching Okinawa. 100,000 Japanese and 50,000 Allied troops lost their lives here, at the bloodiest battle in the World War II Pacific Theatre, Hacksaw Ridge.

During our quick re-fueling stop in Okinawa, officers would give their mission debriefing, and crews would unload our unused ammo that could be used by incoming vessels.

We moved on to mainland Japan, often called "The Land of the Rising Sun." I don't think anyone was disappointed in Yokosuka:

what a great liberty port! Everyone was in the mood for a celebration: we were at the tail end of our deployment and finally headed home.

Yokosuka had a US Naval base, so the locals were very used to sailors, and very friendly to us. The crew was relaxed and at ease in town, where street after street of bars, restaurants, and souvenir shops lined each block.

These souvenir shops were filled with more of the same stuff as in the other foreign ports, but one thing really caught my eye.

One particular shop had two-piece ivory-handled pool cues for sale, for a mere two dollars each! Back home, these would turn a nice profit. I had spent many an evening back home during my high school days at the local pool hall, and knew that $2 was a steal for these sticks. I bought ten of them, and stored them away until I got back to the states. No tax, no duty. Eventually I was able to sell them for fifteen dollars each.

The Navy itself provided lucrative deals for the enterprising sailor. While in international waters, cigarettes were a paltry 10¢ per pack, with no limits how many you could buy as long as you could safely store them. I loaded up, not so much for consumption, but to resell when I got home. Resale at 25¢ per pack was a snap, and the profit paid for my transportation home, plus a little spending money, too! On Saturday mornings at home I would visit my friends and relatives and sell the goods. Everyone made out.

We spent a week in Yokosuka, doing more sightseeing than working. Towards the end of our time here, one evening was devoted to our ships party, held on the base in recognition for our almost-completed tour of duty. The crew felt relieved to be heading home, and it was nice to celebrate back on land. We left on December 14th and started our journey back to the states.

14

Heading Home: Christmas in Hawaii
December 1967

After a quick re-fueling stock at Midway Island, it was clear sailing from Midway Island to Pearl Harbor. While not on watch, we spent the days making needed repairs and sprucing up the ship for our arrival back in the states.

We would often see flying fish during the day traveling alongside the *DuPont*. Approximately 12" long, they had wing-like fins that allowed them to skim above the water for a time before returning to the ocean. On occasion they would land on the deck of the ship.

The nights on the ship were tranquil. In the middle of the ocean, with no lights for hundreds of miles in any direction, the sky was spectacularly clear, and we could see a million stars.

One evening as I was getting off of the 8pm-12am evening watch, my relief from 1st Division said, "I brought you something from the mess decks." I thanked him for the provision as he handed it to me, until I realized it was a flying fish he grabbed off the deck on his way up to the bridge! Startled, I quickly threw it overboard. It was these little acts of kindness that kept us all sane during our extended time overseas.

It took us eight days of steaming to arrive back at Pearl Harbor. It had only been six months since our last visit, but it felt like an eternity to many of us.

We pulled into Pearl Harbor a couple days before Christmas. Even though we were still several thousand miles from mainland USA, it was good to be back in the States once again. Hawaii at Christmas felt kind of strange: I wasn't used to 80° in December!

After a couple of uneventful days in Pearl Harbor taking on food and fuel, we were off to San Diego.

15

Homeward Bound
January 1968

We left Pearl Harbor on schedule with seven days of steaming to arrive in San Diego around New Years Eve, 1967. At this point, the days of week didn't really matter to the crew. We were all just looking forward to getting to home port, and it couldn't come soon enough.

The *DuPont* spent a couple of uneventful days in San Diego taking on more food and fuel before heading south to the Panama Canal once again. After another complete fresh-water power-wash in the lake, we were back in the Atlantic Ocean on the final leg of our deployment.

My hometown buddy Greg Shevick was now a Yeoman, and worked in the ships office. A couple days before we pulled into port, he told me that I should obtain an International Driver's License when we arrived at Norfolk.

He reminded me that since we were the flagship of our squadron, the Commodore was on board. His personal driver was finishing up his tour of duty and there would be need for a replacement. As far as Greg knew, no one currently on the ship had an International Driver's License, which was needed to get that job.

"So if you have that license, you should be a shoo-in!" Even back then, I knew a piece of good advice when I heard it.

When we pulled into Norfolk, the first thing I did was go to the base's office to fill out the proper form and take the test. I was told to check back with them in a week or so, and they would let me know the results.

After a week, I found out that I had passed the test and was presented with my International Driver's License! Sure enough, a couple days later there was a notice in the plan of the day that the *DuPont* was in need of a driver to chauffeur the Commodore to and from the ship each day, and that anyone with an International Driver's License was to report to the ship's office.

When I let them know that I had the credentials they were looking for, the First Class Yeoman in charge looked at me, a little surprised, and said that he would let me know in a week.

Another week went by, and there was a ship-wide announcement that I should report to the ship's office. The First Class Yeoman in charge told me that I was T.A.D.[1] and would be reporting to the Commodore's office every day. I had become his designated driver just like that.

------

[1] Tour of Additional Duty

I received my temporary orders and brought them down to the 1st Class boatswain's mate, who was not happy to lose someone every time we pulled into port.

No more paint locker duty, was my first thought. While still attached to 1st Division, my dockside duty was to be ready whenever the Commodore needed to go somewhere.

My responsibilities included picking him up in the morning, dropping him off somewhere for lunch, and taking him back to the ship at the end of the day – and once he was where he needed to be, I had a car to go wherever I wanted in port! Nobody else on the ship had that kind of privilege.

Me and Greg Shevick (left) in the Yeoman's office

Upon returning to Norfolk, the *DuPont* was like a ghost town. Everyone who wanted leave took it for at least a week or more. Many sailors were also finished with their enlistment and were released from duty. Others were transferred to other ships or duty stations, and replacements began to arrive as fast as those leaving. Soon many of the divisions had turned over half of their crew. After a month and a half or so of this transition, the *DuPont* was ready for more operations, this time in the Caribbean.

16

Caribbean Travels
Spring 1968

Compared to an eight-month deployment to Vietnam, a two-month Caribbean cruise was nothing. Caribbean operations were vastly different, and much more relaxed, than our West Pac trip.

While still attached to 1st Division while out at sea, I had relinquished my paint locker responsibilities. They needed someone who was full time 1st Division, and that was no longer me. I often wondered what the new recruit given the job thought of his role.

In addition to the many new recruits, we were assigned a group of midshipmen (*plebes[2]*) from Annapolis Naval Academy. Time aboard a Navy vessel during summer break is part of their training to get prepared for life as an officer upon graduation.

There were probably twenty plebes on board, spread throughout the ship in different divisions, and they rotated every

---

[2] First-year Annapolis cadets.

couple of weeks to get a taste of all operations aboard the ship. It was great having these guys on board – they did our work for us!

In addition to entertaining these midshipmen for six weeks, one of the *DuPont's* prime responsibilities was to prepare for recovery of an *Apollo* command module. Neil Armstrong, Buzz Aldrin, and Michael Collins would not get to the Moon for another year, but all eyes were on the space program in 1968 so this was a very important responsibility.

The *DuPont* was one of the ships standing by to pick up Apollo astronauts in case of an abort shortly after takeoff. We had a mock capsule on board which we would drop off in the ocean, and circle around for a simulated pickup.

After that we would once again drop the capsule into the ocean, circle around, and do a simulated pickup again. Over and over. It seemed like we did this for days on end and consequently spent a lot of time off the coast of Florida preparing for this historic flight.

When the launch date came, we were on-station, with many other ships in the Caribbean, ready to perform a pick-up if needed. Fortunately, this launch went off without a hitch, and after training for a month it was all over in a few minutes. As soon as the rocket passed us, we received word that all systems were good to go and we could head back to home port.

◆ ◆

During this mini cruise, we made stops in several ports new to me, including Puerto Rico, Bermuda and St. Thomas.

St. Thomas was especially interesting. We anchored out in the harbor, because the pier wasn't able to accommodate a ship of our size. As I was still the Commodore's Driver, I was told to get my bathing suit ready: I was taking the Commodore and a couple other officers to a place called Magens Bay when we dropped anchor. There was a water taxi waiting for us and a car at the pier.

One of the officers knew the way, and in no time we were sitting in one of the most beautiful beaches I had ever seen. *This is living*, I thought. While everyone else was on the ship, I got to relax on a beach with a drink.

All together the ship's crew spent a couple days in St. Thomas with ample time off. I recall one evening, returning to the pier to take the taxi back to the ship. A couple shipmates were chatting about how far out the ship was from where we were. My buddy Walter Keeton said, "It doesn't look that far," bragging that he could swim to the ship. Before we knew it, he had jumped off the pier and swam back to the *DuPont!* He went before the Captain for that stunt, but avoided major punishment.[3]

---

[3] In 2010, I met with Walter for lunch, and spent some time discussing life on the DuPont. When the conversation got around to our stop in St. Thomas, I asked him, "Do you remember one evening that some asshole jumped in the water off the pier and swam back to the ship?" "Do I remember it?" he replied, "That was me!"

Years later, at one of our reunions, he recounted some additional details. As he tells it, the ship was anchored about a mile from the ship! Under the cover of darkness, with the distance, water taxis to avoid, and even sharks in the harbor, it was a miracle he wasn't killed in that stunt.

A fair amount of new sailors meant there was a lot of training to do once we left port, and our division was on a 4-section watch load (one full night of sleep every four days).

But the time went quickly, and before we knew it we were back home to Norfolk.

The summer of 1968 was full of civil unrest back home and all across the country. Martin Luther King Jr. was assassinated in April, and Robert Kennedy that same June!

Fortunately for us, none of the demonstrating or racial tension that now defines the late '60s made its way to the rank & file of our ship. While there were no people of color in the *DuPont's* officer ranks, several of the Chief Petty Officers[4] were black, and they were often the most professional of all our duty chiefs.

I can't recall one single incident on board that caused any problems for us. Race, political affiliation, or even what we thought about the war didn't come into play. We were all Navy Sailors and got along fine. After all, there wasn't enough room on the ship to be picky with where you slept or who you ate with, and all the jobs on a ship are equally lousy.

We were mostly buffered from the stuff that was going on outside of the military at the time, whether it was demonstrations against the war or civil unrest. We would get occasional reports about the problems in cities back home, but it wasn't a steady stream of news to give us anxiety: shipboard life in combat zones was stressful enough. I am sure that there were lots of concerns

---

[4] Enlisted, career sailors with seniority.

for our families, but it never came to a head on board, and was rarely mentioned. Everyone had a job to do on the ship, and that was that.

By the 4th of July, we had made it to Wilmington, Delaware. The ship received word that she was to return to Vietnam, leaving in a month.

With a month to get ready for another Western Pacific deployment, many of the sailors who had leave coming quickly requested it, myself included. My tenure as Commodore's Driver was now coming to an end as well, and it looked like I would be back on the deck force full time once again, something I wasn't looking forward to.

There was a great deal of turnover on the *DuPont*, now that we were going to be deployed for another extended period.

There happened to be opening in the supply division for a ship serviceman[5]. By this time I was well-connected around the ship, and the supply officer and I got along well. He recommended me for this position, and a couple weeks later I was in training to be a ship serviceman, very grateful for the opportunity, but even more thankful to finally be out of 1st Division. By the end of August 1968 we left Norfolk Virginia on our second West Pac tour, and we all wondered what lay ahead of us.

---

[5] A fancy term for "a guy doing laundry for the crew."

Interlude

Comments on an East Coast Destroyer's Vietnam Tours - Second
Deployment
CDR R. H. Small, USN, Commanding Officer USS DuPont (DD941)

*During the first thirty days after return to homeport, ships are
usually left pretty much alone to allow granting a maximum of leave
lend liberty. Almost immediately on tying up to the pier, men with
orders were transferred, replacements began arriving and the long,
slow process of training new men commenced prior to resuming the
very active Atlantic Fleet schedule. This one month grace period was
quickly followed by a two month deployment to the Caribbean, an
Apollo Space craft recovery mission, and a Fourth of July port visit to
Wilmington, Delaware, the land of the DuPonts.*

*It was during this visit that the ship received word that she was to
return to Vietnam, leaving the next month as a last-minute
replacement for a ship that had major mechanical problems.*

*Such short notice for redeployment to WestPact caused major
problems in manning, training, and supply. To ensure that the crew
had enough remaining time to complete this second cruise, seventy
percent of the officers and men were replaced. Drafts of men were
hurriedly sent aboard, many straight from boot camp, some from
Navy Brigs, but the largest percentage were volunteers from within*

74

the destroyer force. Fifty-two men reported on board the day the ship departed, 23 August 1968. Two men caught up with the ship in Long Beach, California.

17

A.W.O.L.
August - September 1968

With our second deployment to Vietnam imminent, I took a week's leave to see friends and family before it started. Up until this point I had been planning on attending my brother's wedding in mid-September, but that all changed with our new orders. My family was understandably disappointed in my not being able to attend, but with me being in the military, they knew that sacrifices were necessary.

With all of the new recruits coming aboard, I figured that plenty of them had no idea how to stretch their measly monthly allowance. With almost two years in, my monthly take-home pay was probably double what the new recruits were getting, so I made some extra withdrawals from the bank. My slush fund account was now nicely padded and ready.

With only a little more than a month to prepare for this upcoming tour, there was lots to do. It seemed like preparations were endless. The ship had to be completely painted before our departure, and I thanked God that I was out of 1st Division and now a ship's serviceman.

My duty was pretty cut and dry. I worked a regular shift in the laundry room learning the finer points of washing, drying, and ironing clothes for the crew. My teacher was a seasoned 1st Class Petty Officer who quickly showed me how to cut corners and make my job easier. This was a far cry from the 1st Class Boatswains Mate in 1st Division that made everyone's life difficult.

Soon enough, August 23rd rolled around and we once again headed for the coast of Vietnam. The day we departed, 52 men, sailors who were either transferred from another duty station or were new recruits fresh out of boot camp, reported aboard the *DuPont*.

This second tour was routine for the sailors that had made the first trip, but there was a lot of training for the new guys. Out at sea, my routine didn't change. I worked my shift in the laundry room and spent a lot of time watching my buddies from 1st Division train our new recruits.

We transited through the Panama canal zone without incident, gave the *DuPont* another fresh water wash, and before we knew it, we were back in the Pacific Ocean once again. We arrived in Long Beach, California on Sept. 5th. What was supposed to be a few days to bring on stores and final preparations before heading west was extended: we received notice that the ship needed to have her boilers repaired, and wasn't going anywhere until they were fixed.

So we hung around, day after day waiting for word when the ship was going to be ready to sail once again. By September 10th, I figured if the ship wasn't going anywhere anyway I could get some leave and still attend my brother's wedding.

I put in for leave and was denied. The Captain wasn't granting any, as he didn't know when the ship would be fully operational and ready to get underway. Four days later we were still tied up pier-side and no one seemed to know when we were leaving.

By Friday, September 13th, with the wedding only two days away, I decided to head home and attend the wedding, in spite of the Captain's denial of my leave request. The weekend was fast approaching and I figured they wouldn't miss me for a couple days anyway.

I took a trip to the Yeoman's office and let my buddy Greg know what my plans were. "How are you going to get home?" he asked.

I told him I would take a bus to Los Angeles Airport and hop on a plane to NJ.

"You can't get on a plane without leave papers. I'll type some up for you so you won't have any problem getting home." Were it not for Greg, I would have made it to the airport in my Navy attire, and probably gone straight back to the dock when they refused to sell me a ticket.

After a red-eye on Friday evening and landing safely at Newark airport the next morning, I called home for a ride. The family was overjoyed that I made it home! When I got in, mom wondered how I had gotten leave. I told her the Captain let me take a few days off. "Well, I should send him a box of cookies," she replied, "He is such a nice man."

I wondered what my fate would be when I finally got back on board the DuPont.

I had a day to get ready for the wedding with this cloud hanging over my head, but I couldn't let my situation ruin the wedding, so I kept my cool. Everyone was busy that day anyway.

In the afternoon, there was a knock on the front door. I answered the door to find Western Union, asking for Mr. Perrotti. "I have a telegram from the *USS DuPont*," he told me. I signed for it, and sent him away. *Good thing my dad didn't answer the door,* I thought.

My mom asked, "Who was that?"

"It was a Western Union telegram from the Captain on the ship. He just wanted to make sure I got here okay."

"Oh, he is such a nice man! I have to send him a box of cookies," Mom said, idly, really starting to make me think she would actually do it!

"Don't bother, mom," I told her. After reading over the telegram and seeing the part about *"missing ships movement into a war zone,"* I thought to myself, *I am in hot water now.*

My parents, rest their souls, never knew that I abandoned my ship.

The wedding was a great affair. Sometime during the festivities, I told my cousin that I was A.W.O.L., and tomorrow I needed to get back to my ship. He agreed to take me down to the Philadelphia Naval Shipyard on Monday so I could turn myself in.

I arrived at the Philadelphia Naval shipyard Monday morning and told them what had transpired the past few days, whereupon

I was immediately escorted to the base brig for processing. Stripped down to my skivvies, I guess to make sure I wasn't carrying any weapons, I was given a completely new sea bag of Navy issue clothing. Just what I needed. *With just a little bit more than a year to go until my enlistment was up, I'll never get a chance to wear this stuff*, I thought.

What I am doing in the brig, I pondered the next morning. "There must be some mistake," I told the petty officer in charge. My pleas fell on deaf ears, but the brig isn't actually a jail. It was basically a dormitory with beds on either side and a table in the middle for passing away the time with other sailors in trouble. No hard labor, no calisthenics, just hanging around with nothing to do.

By Wednesday, I had gotten acquainted with these guys and we talked a lot about our time in the Navy. "What are you in for?" I asked each of them in turn. Three guys gave three answers, each one worse than the last:

"I've been on the run for six months, and they finally caught me."

"I set the ship on fire."

"I tried to kill my captain."

Finally it was my turn to confess what got me thrown into the brig.

"I went to my brother's wedding," And everyone got a laugh out of that. *It would be wonderful to get out of this mess,* I thought to myself.

Once Thursday hit, I was getting a little anxious about being away from my ship for almost a week. I found out when they ushered me into the office that the *DuPont* had left Long Beach, California, earlier in the week, and they had nowhere to put me until the ship hit Pearl Harbor.

The *DuPont* was scheduled to pull into port anytime, so they would be sending me back to the ship immediately. I was sent with my new sea bag in tow to the Philadelphia airport, where I boarded a commercial airliner bound for LAX.

Two MPs took me on to the plane (handcuffed, I might add) and instructed the stewardess that I was not to move from my seat without permission. I recall sitting next to a mother and her young son. She seemed a little bit uneasy about being next to someone in handcuffs. After I relayed my tale of woe to her, we got along fine.

When we landed at LAX airport, the pilot, via the PA system, instructed everyone to remain seated until one of the passengers was escorted off the plane. Two MPs boarded and proceeded to take me off the aircraft, again in handcuffs. I was whisked off to the military office at the airport. Several hours later I was on another plane on my way to Hawaii. I went through the same drill from LAX to Hawaii, escorted and handcuffed until I arrived at Pearl Harbor.

As I arrived back on the *Dupont,* dragging my new sea bag with me, I was actually relieved to be home. Crossing the gangplank and arriving on the quarter deck, the messenger of the watch said to me, "Man, Perrotti, you are in trouble." This ordeal was not over yet.

18

A Court Martial En Route to Vietnam
September 1968

After we left Pearl Harbor, proceeding due West back to the Gulf of Tonkin, I went before the Captain to take my medicine for going A.W.O.L in Long Beach. We were out at sea a couple days and my division officer told me at morning quarters we were going to *Captain's Mast*. You are summoned to *Captain's Mast* when you do something that warrants some type of punishment.

As a review for the non-initiated, there are three types of Court Martial.

1) *Summary Court Martial:* by far the lowest level, given for the least serious crimes committed.

2) *Special Court Martial*: this includes a military judge, prosecution and defense counsel, and potentially a jury.

3) *General Court Martial*: the most serious, and includes military judge, trial counsel, defense counsel, and several court members.

Sometimes there are extenuating circumstances where there is no punishment given, and you are dismissed with little more than a reprimand. I was hoping that this was the case for me (it wasn't).

I didn't know it at the time, but two other sailors on the *DuPont* missed ship's movement. I guess they had weddings to go to also!

I went ahead of them, so I had no idea what was about to befall me, and to this day, don't know what their fate was. So, I went before the Captain and he looked me straight in the eye. "You disobeyed a direct order. I told you no one was getting leave, and you went anyway. I am awarding you a summary court martial."

Wow, after two years in the Navy I am finally getting an award!

In a situation like mine, the Captain tells you what he has decided, and he leaves the sentencing & punishment to the officer who oversees the case, which for me took place a couple days after *Captain's Mast*. It was pretty casual, done by one of the department officers on board: just him and me in his state room. I knew this officer by name only: Lieutenant McCann was our Operations Officer. Going in, I was pretty scared, and didn't really know what I was in for.

The Lieutenant said to me, "I heard about what you did, and quite frankly I would have been tempted to do the same thing." He continued, "It says here in your records that in two years you haven't even had one minor infraction, and no extra duty at all.

That's exceptional," he said. For a minute, I thought I was off the hook!

"However, for a Summary Court Martial, there has to be a punishment. I am giving you the minimum punishment allowed."

Phew.

"I am busting your rank from Seaman E-3 to Seaman Apprentice E-2. Your pay is reduced. You will pay for the new sea bag that was issued to you in Philadelphia.[1] You will also be charged for the plane fare from Philadelphia to Hawaii. Finally, you are restricted to the ship for 60 days."

Being restricted to the ship includes all time at sea. Since we were going to be at sea probably 40 days of this or more, this meant that I'd serve most of my time "restricted to the ship" while we were in the middle of the ocean. Not bad.

My rank was reduced, my pay was busted, and I was stuck on the ship. *Thank God for my slush fund!*

We made another stop at Midway Island for fuel and some entertainment from the Gooney Birds. After six more days of steaming we made one last pit stop in Guam before heading to Subic Bay, our last port before heading back to the gun line.

---

[1] The additional sea bag contained a full set of clothing: dress whites & blues, work clothing, caps, socks, a peacoat, and more. In the end, I made money renting out my surplus clothing from this bag when other guys needed something for an inspection.

Being a ship's serviceman overseas had its perks. It didn't matter what shape you were in (or your uniform was in) when you returned to base, just that you were presentable when leaving. Since you weren't getting liberty if you didn't have a pressed uniform when leaving the ship, I had a lot of requests by sailors to iron their uniforms so they could go on liberty before pulling into Subic. At $4 per uniform to get your whites pressed, this laundry room gig was turning out to be pretty good.

Next stop, the coast of Vietnam.

19

Gun Line Tour #2
October 1968

Once again, we were on the way to Vietnam, resuming gun line duty. This time, we would patrol the entire coast of Vietnam. Our missions were varied: The *DuPont* offered gunfire support to the Marines and Army inland, as well as the Navy Seals, Swift Boats, and the Coast Guard.

We had tremendous support from other ships on patrol with us, most notably the *USS New Jersey BB-62*. She was re-commissioned in April 1968, and after being deemed battle-ready was immediately sent to Vietnam.

The *New Jersey* offered gun fire support to the troops inland as well, and we operated in close proximity to one another many times over the next four months.

Once during this tour, I recall the Captain announcing at morning quarters, "In a couple days we will come alongside the *New Jersey* to exchange documents via high line. She is the pride of the Navy, and we want to make a good impression during

this exchange. I want everyone at quarters[1] and in white hats."
Typically at sea, we were allowed to wear ball caps, but not this
time.

When the moment finally came for rendezvous with the mighty
New Jersey, we were far from the coast, and it was noon. The
DuPont's crew was at quarters. As we approached, we saw that the
New Jersey was not observing the same decorum: shirtless sailors
lounging around, guys napping on the gun mounts. Only one
small station was manned amidships to send and receive
documents. We all got a good laugh at that, as did the *New Jersey*.

During more serious times, when we were on gunfire support
ops, we had the chance to see the *New Jersey's* mighty guns in
action. Even though we were far enough to not be in any danger,
we could hear her 16" guns exploding. The sounds were
deafening, and the accuracy was uncanny. She would operate
10-15 miles off the coast, fire inland, and still hit her targets. A 20-
mile range was inconceivable to most of us (remember, the
DuPont's maximum range was about thirteen miles).

Having the *New Jersey* on patrol with us took the pressure off the
crew of the *DuPont*. Veterans of our prior tour could feel the
difference, but regardless, after 30 days on the gun line, we were
ready for some liberty.

---

[1] At attention

20

Liberty Call:
Subic Bay & Sasebo, Japan
November 1968

We left the gun line on November 4th, watching the *USS New Jersey* pelt the coast of Vietnam. After one quick stop in Subic Bay for a day, it was onto Sasebo Japan for extended liberty of 10 days. Sasebo hosts a Navy base and we were tied up pier-side, which made it easier for us to get to town. With my time under restricted movement over, I looked forward to some dry land (and saki). As it turned out, saki wasn't to my liking, so it was back to beer and mixed drinks.

On the base, there was a major Navy PX[1] where sailors could purchase as much as they could afford to buy. All kinds of stuff – fine China, knives, stereos – for sale with no tax, no duty, and at cheap prices. How could we resist these bargains? But one of the problems we had aboard a relatively small ship was storing stuff. We managed, but space was getting tight. More on that later.

---

[1] Post Exchange

◆◆

Sasebo was filled with a mixture of bars, restaurants with American names, and souvenir shops. Being in port for an extended amount of time is great to get familiar with the town and your favorite places to go. My friends and I found a local bar and got to know the owner pretty well. Outside this particular bar there was a hot dog stand, and one evening I stopped to ask the stand owner how he was doing, not really expecting an answer.

"Fine, thank you! How are you?" he responded, in perfect English! I was blown away by this guy's command of our language. We struck up a conversation and I learned about his background. He was born in the states and moved back to Japan when he was a child, but his parents wanted him to retain the language. I was very impressed, to say the least. As a kid from Elizabeth, keeping current with two languages didn't seem like an easy task.

After going back to our favorite watering hole for a few days, the owner of the bar asked us if we would like to take an afternoon off to see some of the Japanese countryside, and we jumped at this opportunity.

We spent a relaxing day traveling through the city and out into the rural areas of Japan through some nearby cities, taking in the scenic views. Eventually, we stopped at a park and got out for a walk. Our friend hadn't told us where we were headed until we came to bridge overlooking an open field.

"This," he said, "was where the Americans dropped the bomb on Nagasaki that ended the war."

The small group of us, mostly under twenty years old, just stood there, dumbfounded. We had all grown up knowing of the war that came before us (only twenty-three years prior), but what could we say? My father had fought during WWII, but didn't have particular love for talking about his time in the Army.

Our friend didn't seem to be looking for any type of apology. I think he just thought it was someplace we would want to see. The rest of the day was uneventful.

21

Gun Line
Nov. 28th - Dec. 19th

This particular three-week rotation went without incident, full of routine patrols and gunfire support. As the *DuPont* did not need to fire as many rounds each rotation as our first tour, the ship was holding up pretty well this time around.

On some evenings, while anchored out in Da Nang harbor, we could see explosions inland, and special illuminating rounds lighting up the sky. These rounds were designed to produce light to illuminate a target area. Tracer rounds were used, too. These would create a line of sight that allowed the marines inland to track the trajectory for accuracy. This line was also a direct path to us, which could be very unnerving! Luckily, we got through all this unscathed and all hands were looking forward to our next liberty port. At least we wouldn't be spending Christmas out at sea! We departed the gun line once again on December 19th, and headed back to one of our favorite ports of call: Kaohsiung, in Taiwan.

22

Liberty in Kaohsiung, Taiwan
Christmas 1968 - New Years Day 1969

Two days after leaving the gun line, we arrived in Kaohsiung, Taiwan once again. Being away from home during the holidays was bad enough, but having to spend it out at sea would have been horrible. At least we would be in port over Christmas and New Years.

It had been over a year since the *DuPont* last visited this port, and I wondered if there had been many changes.

This port was a regular stop for all naval vessels operating off the coast of Vietnam. The proximity (about 900 miles from Da Nang) made it convenient for ships to get there quickly after finishing a rotation: one ship would leave, and another would take its place in the harbor the same day. Consequently, the town had a steady stream of sailors every day looking to spend their money.

Nothing much changed here over one year. The bars were the same, as were the restaurants and souvenir shops. On a prior visit to Kaohsiung, there was a Buddha statue that caught my eye, and there were still plenty for sale. My buddy Greg and I looked at these, and knew we had to purchase them. Hand-carved out of teak wood, they stood about 4 feet tall, weighing 45 pounds. What a great souvenir this would be! On our previous stop in Kaohsiung, I would have had nowhere at all to store a statue that I carted back to the ship. I wasn't sure if I would have a place this year either, but took a chance and purchased it. As a Yeoman, Greg had a place to stow his. Dragging these back to the ship was a chore, and with our new, prized possessions sitting next to us in the water taxi, we got crazy looks from the other sailors who were also returning (no doubt, jealous of our new friends).

Back on board, crossing the quarterdeck, my division officer had the watch. "Perrotti," he barked, "what is that, and where are you going to keep it for the next three months?"

I told him I would find a place for it, and it wouldn't be in the way. As it happened, this Buddha wound up in my rack, and I spent many a night sleeping on the 02 level under the stars on our way back to Norfolk.

Being in port this long, especially around the holidays, was a festive time, and my shipmates liked to spend money celebrating. Since they had a tendency to run out of cash, suddenly there was a higher demand for loaned cash. On this occasion, the rate went up from our customary $10 today for $14 next week, to $10 today at a payback of $15 next week. The borrowers didn't seem to mind this at all and neither did us lenders.

One afternoon, I noticed one of our shipmates leaving the *DuPont* with his seabag – this was not a good sign. He was a gunner's mate, and a regular customer of mine. I asked one of the other gunner's mates working on the mount near me, "What's up with Stevens?"

"Oh, he has a case of hepatitis and is on his way to the hospital ship. We won't see him again."

I guess I won't ever see my $30 either, I thought. As it turned out that was the one and only time I didn't get paid back.[1]

After celebrating the New Year in town, we once again left Kaohsiung, bound for the gun line. On the way out, there were ships waiting to take our place in the harbor.

---

[1] Forty years after my time in the US Navy, I often wondered what happened to all of my former *DuPont* shipmates. So I decided to start the search, and was able to get in touch with a few of them. Some wanted no part of my idea of getting back together with the old crew. Others, I was never able to find a trace of, but I did have a reasonable amount of success, so I kept at it. I recall one particular call I made was to Stevens: I introduced myself and asked him if he remembered me and his days on the *DuPont*. To my delight, he remembered vividly his time with us.

"I remember a lot about that time as well," I said. "In fact, I seem to recall that you contracted hepatitis in December 1968, and had to be taken off of the ship."

He whistled. "Damn, Perrotti, you sure do have a good memory!"

My memory also recalled the thirty dollars, but I couldn't bring myself to mention that to my newly-reunited shipmate, and just let it go at that.

23

Unreps & Liberty: Hong Kong
Jan 1969

After a day or two of steaming, we were back into the thick of things once again. This tour of duty was more than half over now, so we were on the downside, continuing to operate off the coast, offering gunfire support to the troops inland. This particular rotation was to be a mere sixteen days, basically half of a standard rotation. We followed the six on / six off watch rotation plus unreps to take on fuel, food and ammo.

Unreps involved pulling alongside our supply ship and maintaining station-keeping. They would shoot a line across the water to our ship, which we would grab and pull: it eventually became the line with which we would transfer material or fuel. This could be tricky business, especially in rough seas (or at night, when the schedule required).

Once particularly nasty night, our fuel line was ripped from the ship before the tanks were topped off. With hundreds of gallons of diesel fuel spewing all over the deck, into the sea, and all over us, those clothes were thrown overboard as soon as that detail was over. I can still smell it.

At least once we had to abort an unrep due to high seas. There are many memories of my time in Vietnam that I look back and smile about, but I can still remember nervously eyeing a one-ton pallet of projectiles as it swung back and forth across our deck during a rough night at sea: this was not *In the Navy* with Abbot & Costello, that was for sure!

Unrepping shells

After a while, however, these unreps became routine for the crew, and before we knew it, we were once again heading back to Hong Kong for some much needed liberty.

◆◆

One of our favorite ports of call during the two *DuPont* Western Pacific tours of duty was, without a doubt, Hong Kong. This round, we were there for approximately one week, with as much liberty granted as we needed. The locals were very used to American sailors, and treated us well.

As in any big city there are dangers. We were told (more than once) to stay together, and also given areas which were off-limits, though MPs patrolled the bars and restaurants regularly. I guess we felt that there was never any real danger to us as long as we ran in packs.

Many of my shipmates could be found at the one of the custom tailors throughout the city: everyone wanted to look good upon their arrival back in Norfolk in less than three months. Others spent their time at the local bars and restaurants. I did both.

On January 28th, 1969 it was time to say good by to Hong Kong, and head back to the gun line for one final rotation.

24

Gun Line: The DuPont's Final Round
January-February 1969

We arrived back on the gun line around January 30th. This final round lasted 13 days, the shortest patrol of our tour. Whether this was due to the *DuPont's* fatigue or the support from other ships operating with us didn't much matter: we were only a short two weeks from starting our journey home.

Operating with the *New Jersey* again was a welcome relief, taking the strain off of every ship operating in the Gulf of Tonkin.

The *New Jersey* fired over 5,500 16" rounds and more than 14,000 5" rounds in support of our troops inland. But after this cruise, her work was over and in December 1969 she was decommissioned once again.

As for the *DuPont*, her gun line duties this tour totaled over 75 days patrolling the coast, offering gunfire support to our troops. On this cruise, she fired over 10,000 rounds of ammo. Over two deployments she spent a total of over 160 days on the gun line expending over 30,000 rounds. At this point she was ready to head back to the states, but not before several more ports for more liberty.

We left the gun line for the very last time on February 12th, and headed back to our favorite home away from home, Subic Bay.

25

Subic Bay, Philippines: en route to the Equator
February 1969

After our final stop in Subic Bay for five days of leave, during which my shipmates spent freely at our most frequently visited port, the *DuPont* set off due south toward Australia and New Zealand.

After two or three days out at sea we were back to normal ship's routines. I wasn't standing bridge watches any longer as my duties were confined to the laundry room, which was fine with me: I did my shift and had ample time off.

Being a laundry man has many perks. Coming back on board after liberty, a sailor's uniform is sometimes unfit to be worn again without washing, so he throws it into the laundry bag. If it happens that he forgets to empty his pockets, the money gets... laundered. I can't tell you how many times I found change, and bills too! The first time money rolled out of the dryer, I foolishly tried to find its rightful owner.

I returned to the division with their freshly washed uniforms and got their attention. "Anyone lose any money?" Imagine my surprise when the whole division raised their hand! Of course, nobody could recall how much. So that was how I found one last revenue stream on the way back home.

Curiously there was a lot of activity on the fantail of the ship during this leg out on the open pacific. Loads of preparation, for *something*. Sailors were building giant bins and containers that looked like coffins, and instead of throwing the our food waste overboard (as was customary), the garbage was winding up in these new caskets. All this activity (by veteran sailors alone) was starting to make the crew nervous. Something was up for sure.

It took us twelve days of steaming to reach the land "down under," but before we arrived, we had to cross the Equator, be initiated into King Neptune's Kingdom, and become a Shellback.

26

From Pollywog to Shellback: Crossing the Equator
February 22nd, 1969

For over 400 years, naval vessels have observed a rite of passage for Pollywogs (sailors that have never crossed the equatorial line). Probably 80% of the *Dupont's* crew were Pollywogs, and we were in for it.

Somewhere north of Australia I crossed the Equator and became a Shellback with the rest of the crew, but not before going through one of the most unforgettable experiences in my life.

All Pollywogs are initiated: no one, not even the Captain, is exempt from this tradition. Established Shellbacks were the ones in charge. The initiation varies somewhat from ship to ship, but the *DuPont's* ceremony started innocently enough on our bow.

Everyone was paraded on their hands and knees, in nothing but their skivvies, to the stern of the ship, periodically getting blasted with cold hoses. Next, we went before *King Neptune* to get initiated, who was Dressed in some kind of king's garb with a mop on his head and a trident in one hand.

We were each interrogated by the king, and charges were levied against us. Everyone had a charge: asking for seconds in the chow line, parting your hair on the wrong side, always having pressed work clothes and thus making the rest of the crew feel inferior.

They charged me with twirling my mustache too often, and I was guilty as charged, as was everyone else brought before the king.

Some special, predetermined sailors got the maximum sentence, and I happened to be one of them.

My sentence included *kissing the royal baby's belly.* The biggest guy on the ship had slathered his belly with axle grease, and all the initiates put their face into his gut. It was as disgusting as it sounds.

After that, I found out what they were saving three days of garbage for.

Part of my sentence included wallowing around in the coffin they had made especially for this occasion, filled with three days of food waste. Next, I had to gargle a concoction of soy sauce and oil.

Finally, I went into the pool to wash off. If you were one of the first in line, going into the pool wasn't so bad. After a while, though, all of the garbage wound up in the pool, which got as disgusting as you can imagine. When the ceremony was over, we were all thoroughly washed down. All in good fun, but it was controlled chaos for sure.

When it was finally over, I had been duly initiated into *The Solemn Mysteries Of The Ancient Order Of The Deep,* and was officially a Shellback.

With this time-honored ritual behind us, we set our sights towards Australia.

27

Liberty Call: Australia and New Zealand
March 1969

A day or so after crossing the equator, things got back to normal aboard the *DuPont*. We headed south toward our next destination: Sydney, Australia. On the way, we passed several islands and were treated to history lessons about their significance during World War II. Finally, we arrived in Sydney on the 1st of March. Several shipmates commented about how nice it would be to arrive in a foreign port where English is the spoken language: everyone figured we would have no problems communicating with the locals.

Though it was a foreign country, Sydney was the most like "home" that any of us had seen in months. Word got around that some soldiers who got a week or two away from Vietnam in a place like Australia just decided not to go back to the front lines, and attempted to disappear here. Without a language barrier, it was tempting to a certain portion of enlisted men. More than

106

once, we were warned: don't even think about going A.W.O.L here and missing ship's movement. Someone from every branch of the US Armed Forces had tried it already. Each one was caught, and severely punished.

We got lots of early liberty here, with plenty of time to see the city and sights that Sydney had to offer. The locals seemed to love having us yanks spending all of our money.

We even took in a cricket match! Despite how it looked, cricket was nothing like our national pastime, baseball, but it was fun to watch.[1]

We toured the local world class zoo, and even saw an Aborigine in town. One afternoon, a couple of us met an expat at one of the downtown pubs. An American who grew up in Detroit, he had visited Australia five years before and decided to stay! Like our friend in Sasebo, he asked us if we would like to see some of the sights outside Sydney. As before, we jumped at the chance.

He took us out to tour the countryside. After a few hours, our crew decided to get something to eat, so we stopped at a roadside stand, the kind place where you would order your food and take it outside to eat. "Don't bother to order the hamburgers," he cautioned, as they didn't compare well to the ones in the US.

---

[1] When I began reuniting with my shipmates many years after the events of the war, I was informed just how embarrassing I was at the cricket match. "nothing like baseball" was for sure, but I apparently acted just like one of the worst baseball fans around, with how much I mocked the game, the players, and the whole idea of one of Australia's most-played sports.

Of course, I didn't listen to him. *When in Rome,* right? One bite, and I understood that our Australian buddy knew what he was talking about. "What kind of meat is this?" I asked.

"Kangaroo. Stick with the chicken and you will be okay."

We toured a bit more of the outskirts of town and headed back to the city for another round of drinks and entertainment.

On our last night in port, we were at one of the local pubs and I met a sailor from the *H.M.A.S. Melbourne,* an Australian Naval aircraft carrier that was in port that week as well. After a few beers and some conversation, he mentioned to me how much he admired our white hats and asked if could try mine on. "I would love to have one of these," he said, donning our standard-issue cap.

Meanwhile, his cap fascinated me too! With an extra sea bag full of gear back on the ship, I wasn't going to miss one white hat, so I offered an exchange. We traded hats and went on our way.[2]

When I got back to the ship and crossed the quarterdeck to board, the officer in charge told me that I was out of uniform. "So is the guy who has my hat, I guess!" We had a good laugh at that. He said that I was okay, just to stow that hat and get back in uniform.

During our time in Syndey harbor, the ship was open to visitors. It was a nice change of pace, with over 2,000 locals coming on board during our stay in Sydney!

---

[2] I still have that hat.

This city was definitely the highlight of our deployment; I didn't hear one bad word about it from our ship. As we left, more than one sailor said that they'd be back.

Three days later, we pulled into Wellington, New Zealand for more liberty. Nothing quite could compare with Sydney, but this port came close. It reminded us of a mini Sydney; many of the streets in town had a similar flavor, with lots of pubs and restaurants for us to enjoy.

Our first night in port, the locals held a dance in our honor, at a hall adjacent to our pier. The locals challenged us to a softball game, to be held the next day. A lot of us thought that these guys would know nothing about baseball, but they proved us wrong and beat us 7-6!

As this was our last overseas port of call for liberty, many of the crew went all-out and spent every dime they had. Except for the occasional card game on the way home, this was the last time my slush fund got any real action. In another month, we would be back in Norfolk.

28

Pago-Pago
March 1969

Pago-Pago is a nondescript remote island due north of New Zealand and north east of Australia, easily considered the middle of nowhere. Because of its location, it is a regular refueling stop for commercial and naval vessels who are heading toward or away from Australia or its neighbors.

As we pulled into this tropical island, gorgeous beaches beckoned us. This was to be a quick refueling stop, and then back out to sea on the same-day. The Captain announced that we would be here for several hours, and anyone not on duty who wanted to go for a swim could do so at the beach several hundred yards away. Many sailors took advantage of this, including myself and my buddy Greg, who accompanied me.

At the beach, there was a place to purchase some refreshments. While Greg and the other sailors readied themselves to go swimming, I decided to stay on the beach and have a few drinks. Bidding these a guys "see you later," I relaxed with some cold beer, while nine of my shipmates went out for a swim.

After a only short time out in the water, one of the local Samoans on the beach saw that the sailors were in some trouble with the undertow. The current was fierce, and all the men were suddenly in imminent danger.

Six of my friends were fortunate enough to survive with help from the island locals, but Greg and two others were taken under and out to sea by the current.

What started out as a quick refueling turned into a major tragedy. The *DuPont* stayed moored to the pier overnight waiting for word on the fate of the missing sailors. Nothing.

After surviving two tours of duty off the coast of Vietnam, these men drowned on an afternoon swim break on the last stop before getting back to the states.

In the morning we raised anchor and set sail once again for Pearl Harbor.[1]

---

[1] I went to visit with Greg's father when I got home. He was never able to fully accept his son's death, even after seeing the official ship's report on the incident. He eventually flew to Pago-Pago himself in an attempt to get additional answers. I don't believe he learned anything new, but hopefully that trip helped him gain some closure.

Interlude

Comments on an East Coast Destroyer's Vietnam Tours - Factors Effecting Success

CDR R. H. Small, USN, Commanding Officer USS DuPont (DD941)

Since 1965 a rather large number of destroyers, both Atlantic and Pacific based, have become graduates of the Vietnam gunline "school of hard knocks". DuPont, however, was more successful than most. The question then follows as to why this was so.

Warships are an anachronism for democratic societies. They are by necessity structured to be autocratic institutions. Their Captains are given authority and responsibility for making almost continual judgements and decisions which directly control the lives and possible deaths of every man aboard. Combat action for a naval ship is simply a logical progression to a slightly higher level of risk routine than that which has been in effect during the ship's life until then. In actual fact many non combat situations aboard a ship are more terrifying than most combat.

DuPont *during her deployments to WestPac lost more men to accidents than to enemy fire. (Three men drowned in American Samoa on the ship's return from the last deployment). This fact, then, tends to put a very high premium on pre-action training and performance. Ships that are well motivated and effective peacetime operators will most likely be effective in combat.*

29

The Long Ride Home
March 1969

It would be seven days of steaming before port in Pearl Harbor. With the shock of losing three shipmates fresh on our minds the crew was subdued, and not in the mood you would expect for a bunch of guys on their way *back* from a deployment. We carried on normally as best we could, standing watch and getting the ship ready for our return to Norfolk in less than a month.

We had nightly movies on the mess decks, but if it was particularly nice out, the movie was shown above-decks. I didn't think the movies were all that great: my 4-foot wooden Buddha from Taiwan was still occupying my rack, so I was still sleeping on those decks most nights. You try to sleep while a spaghetti western is blaring for an audience of rowdy sailors right around the corner!

If the crew wasn't watching a movie, you could always find a card game or two. Although I had played cards growing up and in high school, I never played a hand against these sharks. However,

I watched a lot of games, and when one of the sailors was out of money I was right there offering him a loan, in case he wanted to stay in to turn his luck around. If he lost again, I would collect on payday. If he won his money back and then some? I would get my loan back in a couple of hours, with standard rates applied of course. In this way, the worst that could happen was waiting a week or two to get paid. There were even a couple games I can recall where my money was covering more than one guy at the table!

We finally pulled into Pearl Harbor. After six months of foreign ports, it was great to once again be on American soil, even though we were still 2,500 miles from California.

As usual, we spent a couple days bringing on food supplies and doing more prep work for our arrival in our home port. A couple days of liberty later, and we bid farewell to Waikiki and Pearl Harbor.

After six more days of sailing, we made it to San Diego and by now, everyone on board was really getting anxious to get home. The time in San Diego was quick. Two days, and once again we were out to sea getting closer to home port.

Every division always provides a minimum amount of crew in case of any unforeseen circumstance, but several sailors put in for leave and flew home rather than finish the trip on the *DuPont*. This was great for the rest of the crew: when the ship finally docked in Norfolk, more sailors could take their time off because there was a rotation of guys coming back from their leave.

We reached the Panama canal after six more lazy days out at sea. One more fresh water wash down for the *DuPont,* and she was clean and ready for the Atlantic Ocean with a mere seven days until home port.

30

Home Stretch into Norfolk, Virginia
April 1969

The last seven days out at sea were the longest. Everyone was loose and relaxed, but being away from home for eight months takes its toll on both the crew and the ship.

Constant fire from the cannons caused vibration throughout the ship, which loosened lighting fixtures, overhead pipes, wiring, and more, causing problems in all areas of the ship. Repair crews were always fixing something somewhere, and if you happened to have the top bunk you would often wake up covered in dust, from something coming loose overhead.

Rumors had been floating around about what the *DuPont's* next challenge would be. Word had leaked out among the senior staff that she might be going up to Boston for an extensive overhaul, which would no doubt set off an exodus of the crew, even before she went to New England.

Many of the sailors, especially the lifers, had homes in and around Norfolk. Having to stay up in Boston, even for a short period, would not sit well with this bunch.

It would be a month or so before we learned what our next assignment would be. If the ship was going up to Boston and the crew would be disbursing it was time to shut down the slush fund. *You will never see these guys or your money again,* I thought to myself.

Somewhere between the Panama Canal and Norfolk, I was called into LTJG[1] Swantz's state room. He was my division officer, we got along well, and I felt that he had always looked out for me. I had no idea what this was all about, but this meeting wound up being one of the most important conversations of my life.

He had my service records on his desk, and immediately went into why I was called in to see him. "It says here that you are getting out of the Navy in October of this year"

"Yes Sir," I replied.

"How would you like to re-enlist?"

"No thanks," I said: I wanted off this tin can as soon as possible.

"Well, you have to make your own decision, but we are offering a $1,500 bonus if you re-enlist." Calculating in my head the extra money I had made in the last two years with all my side hustles, I had easily made more than the $1,500 they were offering me to volunteer for another four years of active duty.

---

[1] Lieutenant Junior Grade, the second commissioned officer rank in the United States Navy

I politely declined.

"Well then, Perrotti, what are your plans?" I told him that I hadn't decided yet, but my time was served, and I was ready to get out.

Me and Lieutenant Swantz (right)

"Have you thought about college?" he asked. My mind jumped back three years to high school, and how I wasn't an ideal student, and certainly not a good enough one to qualify for college.

"No, Sir, I didn't think I was fit for college."

"Perrotti, if you can get accepted into school, I can get you an early out. You'll be discharged at the end of August instead of the

118

end of October, giving you a couple weeks to transition into civilian life before starting school."

"This sounds great," I said. "How do I get started?"

"When we pull into Norfolk, you're scheduled to go on leave? While you are home, schedule your SATs. Get your transcripts from high school, and set up an appointment with a college or two. If you need more leave, I'll get you a few more days off. All I will need is an acceptance letter from a college and I can get you out in August."

I thanked him for the opportunity, and told him that I was going to look into this.

Almost a year before, I had struck up a friendship with one of the storekeepers in the supply division. Gary had come aboard the *DuPont* around June of '68 and was assigned to the supply division as a storekeeper. As we got to know each other, I quickly learned that he already had a college degree. I asked him once why he didn't come in the Navy as an officer. Easy, he had said. He didn't want that responsibility. He just wanted to do his time and be done with it.

Well, I went straight to Gary to discuss my visit with our division officer. "How do I get all of this done and get accepted into college in just four months?" Gary walked me through it, and gave me the confidence that I would do well in college.

In hindsight, I can trace most of my success in life after the Navy directly to these two guys and their help getting into college. I will forever be indebted to Lieutenant Swantz and my pal Gary.

31

Norfolk, Virginia
April 1969

After an eight month deployment, it was a joyous reunion pulling into Norfolk, Virginia. The pier was jam-packed with friends and relatives, all waiting for the ship to come in. My parents, sister and cousin were among them.

As expected, the ship emptied out quickly, and I took a week of leave to start working on what I needed for college. My family was surprised to learn of my plans, but supported them whole-heartedly. My father had said that the Navy would make a man out of me, and I guess he was right! Before the Navy, I never would have considered college.

By my return to the ship, we had indeed been notified that the *DuPont* was being sent up to Boston for an extensive overhaul. More than half of the crew was in the process of being transferred, exiting the Navy, transferring to a new duty station, or was awaiting orders for their next duty station, as was my case. Sadly, this was the end of my little side business. Though very profitable (and a valuable service to my shipmates), I was out of the slush fund business for good.

It would be a few weeks until the ship pulled out of port once again, bound for a temporary home in Boston for the refit. I had never been to Boston, and wondered what that city was like. I would soon find out.

Norfolk had been my home port for a couple of years, but being on two extended deployments during that time, I never really got to see much of the city. But I had heard many times that locals didn't much care for the sailors stationed here, so I wasn't missing much. I was looking forward to heading north: I would be a hundred miles closer to home than I was now.

Weekend leave was often very easy to get before pulling out of Norfolk, and we frequently got off early on Friday (or even Thursday night). I was able to swing this a couple of times and it usually worked out fine.

One particular weekend close to the end of our time in Norfolk, I took a flight home. Newark International Airport was only about five miles from my home... but unfortunately, my flight was to JFK, not Newark. Over an hour by car to home wasn't ideal, but I figured that I would be almost home, and would figure out something when I got there.

It's important to remember that in 1969, the country was really divided over the Vietnam war, and there wasn't the same "support the troops" but "hate the war" sentiment that you often hear today. Sometimes my uniform was an advantage, and others, not so much, but I always wore it while traveling.

Pulling into JFK, I thought, *now what?* As I exited the plane, I approached one of the ticket agents and asked for some assistance getting to New Jersey.

She took one look at me and said, "There is a helicopter leaving for Newark in about fifteen minutes. I think I can get you on there at no charge." Another first for this kid from Elizabeth: a helicopter ride, and at no charge! I jumped at that opportunity and was escorted to the gate. The trip only took about fifteen minutes, but flying over Brooklyn, and seeing the Statue of Liberty from the air is something I'll never forget.

32

Boston
May 1969

The *DuPont* left Norfolk in early May, 1969, and headed north for the Boston ship yards. What was left of the crew would be there perhaps until the end of the month. Our job was to secure the ship and prepare her for a complete overhaul.

This was light duty: no need to maintain her beauty at this point. Most anything that wasn't going to be needed, or used when her overhaul was completed, was removed from the ship. We all had ample opportunities to take what we wanted, as most of this stuff was going right into the dumpster anyway. I picked up a few authentic Navy blankets, and one of the 1st Class Petty Officers gave me one of the official United States flags that the ship flew. Others took chairs, signs, and other memorabilia, but I was a little more picky.

Liberty in Boston was great. Boston's downtown was filled with lots of bars and restaurants, and light duty meant a lot of time off and early liberty. We took advantage of the time off to see what we could of the city.

While stationed in Boston, I took another week of leave to sit for the SATs, get my high school transcripts, and set up a meeting with the admissions officer at a local community college I had applied to.

Taking the SAT after being out of high school for almost three years was nothing short of embarrassing. I was never a scholar, but I was sure reminded of that fact after this exam. The less said about that, the better.

I will never forget my meeting with the admissions counselor at Union County Community College. It was as nerve-wracking as my court martial! He sat looking at my high school records during our hastily-scheduled meeting. "You know," he said, a forlorn look on his face, "you really aren't college material."

There goes my early out, I thought. I knew that my transcripts were nothing to hang on the wall, but after doing so well in the Navy, it was still hard hearing this from someone behind a desk.

"However," he continued, "we are giving all of you Vietnam veterans a chance, and all the help you need.

Here is your acceptance letter. We will see you in September."

Back at the ship, I showed my acceptance letter to my division officer. "I'll get back to you shortly," he said.

A week later, I was notified that I was approved for an early discharge, and was being transferred to the *USS Davis DD-937*. I was to report to her by the end of the month, at a home port of Newport, Rhode Island.

The *DuPont* was unceremoniously decommissioned the last week of May, and what was left of the crew all went their separate ways. That happened to be a holiday weekend, so I headed home before reporting aboard yet another tin can, the USS Davis, to finish out my Navy career.

33

USS Davis DD-937
June 1969

I reported aboard my third destroyer during the first week of June. The *USS Davis DD-937* was the same class destroyer as the *DuPont*, so I knew my way around immediately.

I was assigned to the ship's laundry room because of my experience as a ship's serviceman, working with two other sailors who welcomed me with open arms.

This tour of duty was going to be a piece of cake, as it would only be about twelve weeks. After the past two years on the gunline, loading ammo, unrepping in choppy water, and eating monkey meat on a stick, I figured I could do laundry off the coast of Rhode Island while standing on my head.

We took a quick Caribbean tour and were back in Newport in July. This was my last time out on the open ocean, and I was pretty happy. Traditionally, on a sailor's last tour, he or she throws a possession overboard to be consigned to the sea forever. My working boots had certainly seen better days, so I bid them farewell and kept up with this tradition. Within about six weeks, I would be transitioning back into civilian life.

◆◆

Like everyone else alive at the time, I recall the day that Apollo 11 landed on the Moon.

It was Sunday, July 20th. I had joined one of my new shipmates to take a ride into Providence that evening. We sat at a local gin mill having a couple of beers, watching history being made on TV.

Nearly 400,000 people worked on the Apollo program: the astronauts, the engineers who designed the rockets, the welders who built them, the computers (people who computed calculations), and sailors like me! I thought about our mission the prior year on the *DuPont* as a recovery ship for an Apollo launch, and how I played some small part in humanity's first steps on the moon. Pretty cool stuff.

As we headed back to the ship that evening, it felt good to be part of the military.

34

Honorably Discharged
August 1969

On my last trip home in early August, I came back to base with a car. I wasn't sure which day I was getting discharged, and wanted to be prepared and on my own when I was let out. Having my own transportation allowed me to pack up a little at a time.

August rolled around, and I knew that my time in uniform would be ending soon. Two weeks before my enlistment was up, I was sent to "transition barracks." If your ship is leaving port, this is where you go to get released: you receive your final physical, paperwork, outgoing pay, etc. before getting discharged.

During these two weeks, I had a lot of time to reflect on my tour of duty. I thought about all of the things I learned, the people I met, and the experiences I had.

I recalled the money I was able to save through various Navy incentives: tax free earnings overseas, hazardous duty pay while in a combat zone, extra pay for duty at sea. These extras, plus my other enterprises, netted me a nice balance when I was released from active duty.

On August 29th, 1969, just one week shy of three years of service to my country, my enlistment was finally over, and I headed home.

The ride back to Elizabeth was exhilarating! In just three years, I went from an aimless teenager who just wanted to stay out of the jungle to a college-bound veteran, on my way to start a new chapter in my life.

Epilogue

I never forgot my experiences in the Navy, but they were just one chapter in a long, happy life. While many of my fellow shipmates never really "came home," I believe that my rapid transition from *sailor* to *student* in 1969 prevented me from dwelling on my experiences, and helped me move on to a fulfilling adulthood, happy marriage, and successful career.

It took me about 10 minutes to transition back into civilian life. While I thought I was more than ready to start college, it turned out that I was wholly unprepared.

Easing into college my first year as a part time student was a smart thing to do, and had it not been for my two Navy mentors who guided and encouraged me, I would have never accomplished what I did.

The G.I. bill helped me tremendously: they kept paying, and I kept going. After five years I received a bachelor's degree in marketing, and shortly after receiving my degree, I received a letter from Uncle Sam, offering to pay for an advanced degree, too!

After eight years of hard work, I had an advanced degree that was well worth the effort. Working as a salesman took me from one job to the next over a 12-year period, and in 1986 I was able to start my own company, working independently for the rest of my career.

About the Author

A post wartime boomer, Raymond was born in 1948 in Elizabeth New Jersey, the son of a WW2 veteran, Vito Rocky, and his wife Carmella.

After three years of service, Raymond returned to New Jersey, found employment, and enrolled in college thanks to the GI bill, ultimately earning a master's degree in business at Fairleigh Dickinson University. Raymond worked as an industry salesman for twelve years before starting his own business in 1987, which he runs to this day.

Raymond is married to his wife of 45 years, Virginia. They have three children and six grandchildren.

Made in the USA
Columbia, SC
03 August 2022

64295621R00080